# The Blessing Challenge

# The Blessing Challenge

by
**Leslie Ballew**

In memory of
Taylor Renee Hamilton,
you are forever a beloved friend.
A friendship always filled with careless jokes,
laughter, and love that will never be forgotten.
6/4/1997- 1/10/2014
*"ily5eva"*

# Table of Contents

Leslie Ballew

# Acknowledgement

Along the journey of writing this devotional, I have been blessed with many helpful hands. I would like to thank first off, my Pastor, Jamey Prickett. His encouragement, support, and theological advice helped guide me throughout this project. From simply bouncing ideas off of him to his full proofread for theological correctness, everything he has done has helped in such an enormous way. Secondly, Katie Smith was a huge help in the inspiration behind this book. Before I had even begun to write this devotional, she taught me the importance of finding blessings throughout any circumstance. Her faith throughout her tribulations along with her testimony that she has shared in this book, speak encouragement to me in my lowest points and helped guide my words for others who are in need for such encouragement. Misty Kennedy's continued interest, help, and support to this book has been so fulfilling. She is not only the mother of Taylor and Alyssa but also like a mother to Taylor's friends. She is such a loving woman that I have been blessed to know. Finally, many of my friends, family, and teachers (Mrs. Jackson especially) have shown such an amazing amount of support throughout my time of writing. I am beyond thankful.

Leslie Ballew

# Author's Note:

      I am only a 17 year-old student writing from my own faith experiences. Please keep this in mind as you read this devotional. I have no seminary or counseling degree. My scripture education is simply as far along as my spiritual journey has taken me. This entire book is written from personal experiences. This entire book is a devotional of personal failures and triumphs. Writing this has simply been me opening my heart for God's use. All glory is to him. I am the unequipped, but I believe that does not matter when in the hands of God. I pray he can use me and any of my experiences shared in this devotional to speak his hope and love to you, wherever needed.

# Foreword

## Finding Rainbows in the Rain
### Testimony by Katie Smith

In February of 2010, I had been sick for many weeks, in and out of the hospital, receiving IV antibiotic treatments at home, trying to recover from a terrible bout of flu. By that spring, my wonderful doctor told me that he didn't really know how much longer he could keep patching me up, that I needed to consider a lung transplant. I was totally devastated. I didn't want to think about it, but I knew that I had no choice but to pursue a transplant. While most people wouldn't suffer so from the flu, I was born with Cystic Fibrosis, a disease that causes sticky blockages in the lungs and digestive systems of people affected. Before this particular flu, I had been very healthy by comparison. I had made it through college in just four years and had a successful teaching career. But God saw fit to bring us to our knees at that moment. In a nutshell, I chose not to go for evaluation at Emory in Atlanta even though it was near home. We felt God leading us to the Mayo Clinic in Jacksonville, Florida. That decision led us right into the center of the refiner's fire. For 3.5 years, I waited, wondering if the phone would ring. For the first 2 years of those 3.5 years, Dustin, my husband, stayed in our home in Georgia and worked at his job during the week, then traveled to Jacksonville on the weekends. To say that this time was stressful would be an understatement. But to say any of the things we went through were wasted would be to underestimate God.

In that time, Dustin was injured at work, which pushed him to find a new job here in Jacksonville. It pushed us to sell our home in Georgia so that we could relocate together. Both of those things were immensely painful in the moment. I could not understand why God would keep tightening the screws!

At the very beginning of my transplant journey, a friend of mine was also going through a valley of her own. Her baby had been born at 25 weeks. She and her husband spent 5 months not knowing if their sweet little girl would live long enough to come home with them, much less grow up. She started reading a book called One Thousand Gifts by Ann Voskamp. I decided to pick it up and read it myself. I put it back down many times before I was able to finish reading it. You see, in that book, Voskamp literally began to give thanks for every single little thing that happened to her, good or bad. One day, I started attempting to do the same. It was so very hard at first. A close friend got her transplant soon after she and I became close. I didn't get to see her for almost three months. I had to turn to God then. I didn't have Robin to run to in that moment. I thanked God for her and her transplant; what I really wanted was to be angry that

God was holding out on me. Dustin got burned badly at work and I was 400 miles away. I came unglued. Then I remembered: "Thank God in all things." So I began to thank God for my family here in Florida that came and sat with me; I thanked God for my parents for going to meet Dustin at the hospital in Atlanta when I couldn't be there. I thanked God for my friends here who helped me pick Dustin up from the airport so he could rest and recover in Jacksonville. I thanked God that Dustin wasn't going to be permanently injured or disabled in anyway. The fact that I was still waiting for a transplant began to fade away. I began to live again instead of waiting. I realized that I wasn't on a journey to a destination anymore, that God was using everything along the way, and that He was using me along the way. I began to realize that God is working all around me, and I needed to join Him where He was already working.

I did eventually get a transplant and I am coming up on one year since! Everyday hasn't been easy. For the first 8 weeks, I was miserable; I even, for a moment, questioned the wisdom of our decision! But God has brought so much joy, so many rainbows in the rain, that I know I could never have made a different decision. I have met so many wonderful people. I have had the opportunity to minister to a very dear friend who has not yet accepted Jesus but I have seen Him change her heart already. I have met wonderful people at our new church who truly embody the definition of church and community. I am now involved in a non-profit that offers housing to patients receiving treatment for cancer and transplants at the Mayo Clinic. God brought all this into my life. He has allowed me to join in His ministry. It is everywhere. We are all ministers, everywhere we are.

Being a Christian does not mean that life is without trial. Often, it feels like we suffer more because of our love for Him. I never understood how anyone could count suffering as joy! But I do know now. God loved me enough to put me through the fire so that I could become better for Him. He loved me enough to draw me to Him so that I could experience His true character, so I could know Him not just about Him. My journey is ongoing, just as yours is ongoing. We are never finished until we reach heaven.

I will leave you with two of my very favorite verses that I have cherished throughout this time with God.

> *"Moses answered the people, 'Do not be afraid. Stand firm and you will see the deliverance the Lord will bring you today. The Egyptians you see today you will never see again. The Lord will fight for you; you need only to be still'"* (Exodus 14:13-14 NIV).

> *"So do not be afraid, for I am with you; do not be dismayed, for I am your God. I will*

*strengthen you and help you; I will uphold you with my righteous right hand"* (Isaiah 41:10 NIV).

*"See, I have engraved you on the palms of my hands; your walls are ever before me"* (Isaiah 49:16 NIV).

The Lord's promises are everlasting. He is never broken one. When he says, "do not be afraid," we are not to be afraid. He is going to fight for us. Always.

## Chapter 1

# #Blessed

DAY ONE:

What is happiness? Where does it come from?

I went with my friend Lexi to volunteer with "Church on the Street," a mission organization out of First Baptist Woodstock Church serving and worshiping with the homeless in Downtown Atlanta. I prayed beforehand that God would shake up my heart through this experience and to also open my eyes to something with which I have been struggling. God in his ever faithfulness provided.

While we were there we would go around to different homeless people gathered and begin a conversation. The conversation would usually begin by us asking them how they were or what their story was. Then after a brief conversation we would ask them how we could pray for them.

One man in particular stuck out to me. This man was known by about every volunteer there. He told us his story of how he was in jail for 15 years, and when he got out he was stuck back on the street. He talked about how he was a sad and pathetic man, and all he did was feel sorry for himself. He then told us about how he started to come to Church on the Street and was saved and given hope. He said he found joy despite his circumstance, got a job (he exclaimed he never thought he would have a real job), and how he was about to move into an apartment within the week.

When we asked him how we could pray for him he told us to pray for the joy of life. He was full of the joy of life, and he wished everyone could be as well. He said there is no reason to feel sorry for yourself when the joy of life is available. He spoke of how God changed him in ways he didn't believe possible.

Throughout the week I realized God was revealing to me the importance of understanding the topic of joy and blessings. Life is hard. We encounter circumstances that are out of our control, we fail, we are betrayed, we get hurt, we loose faith, and we are never perfect. These things are all indisputable. Everyone has things in their life that they wish they could change, completely rid themselves of, or claim control over. No one person's life can be compared to another. NO ONE IS COMPARABLE.

We must first understand the concept of happiness. Happiness is the state of feeling or showing pleasure or contentment. Life holds a lot of surprises though so how can we constantly be with pleasure or contentment? Our future is uncharted in our view. The things we experience are different from what we dreamed of as a child. The uncertainty of life and its surprises is vast. It is hard to know what will happen tomorrow, in a week, or years from now.

One concept to grasp is the fact that we only have some control over the circumstances in our lives. This might come from unexpected changes or disappointments. This realization is vital for happiness.

> *"Though I walk in the midst of trouble, you preserve my life. You stretch out your hand against the anger of my foes; with your right hand you save me" (Psalm 138: 7 NIV).*

> *"The righteous person may have many troubles, but the Lord delivers him from them all" (Psalm 34:19 NIV).*

God does not promise a life of happiness; he promises us help when facing troubles. If we face our circumstances by claiming this promise, by clinging to this promise, we will find that we were created to face just the circumstances that we face. We will either conquer the adversity, or we will find contentment with what once was a source of discontent. One of the first things that we must do is recognize that we are the product of an amazing creator. He created us to face much of what we face. By understanding our self worth and the fact that this very self worth can conquer our challenging situations, we will confront times that had been sources of frustration with the confidence that will help us embrace the challenges that once frightened us. As we trust in God's promise to strengthen us for all that we face, we will find that not only will we understand our situation better, but we will also discover much more about ourselves and our remarkable strength that we once underestimated. Our world is filled with joy if we can simply take notice of such. Our prayer should not be for God to take all struggles out of our lies. Our prayer should be for God to reveal the joy that we have lost site of in these struggles.

## DAY TWO:

Blessings. Not one of the uncommon words found within scripture. Not one of the most uncommon words found in our world. During the month of November, this word is probably one of the most common words found in our world. Throughout the year we sprinkle this word into our thoughts frequently. You are getting along with your family, blessed. Your friend gave you a really nice surprise, blessed. You had a good nap, blessed. You scored a good parking spot at Wal-Mart, blessed. People throw this word around constantly throughout their day, usually when things are going good. You can scroll for days looking at tweets with the "hashtag" blessed on twitter. If our society is constantly speaking of blessings and gratitude, why are so many so distressed? Why does our country have such a high percentage of depression, anxiety, and suicide issues? If we know we are blessed with more than we deserve or just what we need, then why does greed, envy, anxiety, and worthlessness

4

haunt our minds? Is it that we do not understand what our blessings are, or are we just too stubborn to acknowledge our blessings as real? Some days when I hear someone speak of their blessings I feel like they are giving what I call "the Sunday School Answer." It is the answer that will make everyone smile and sympathize. Do we understand our blessings as real? DO WE EVEN UNDERSTAND WHAT A BLESSING IS?

I think a word lesson is needed for the people of our generation. According to the Online Etymology Dictionary,

> "This word was chosen in Old English bibles to translate Latin benedicere and Greek eulogein, both of which have a ground sense of 'to speak well of, to praise,' but were used in Scripture to translate Hewbrew brk 'to bend the knee, worship, praise, invoke blessings' . . . Meaning shifted in late Old English toward 'pronounce or make happy,'" (Harper).

So originally this word meant to praise and speak well of. How did the meaning change to our current meaning of bliss and happiness? Along these lines, something that brings happiness is not always something praise worthy. Blessings can come in not so pleasant forms, a fact we often forget. I think our world needs a reality check of what a blessing truly is before we can focus on the blessings in our daily lives.

Now do not get me wrong, I realize the world is a tough place. The world is painfully broken, and that is a fact of life. I do not think that gratitude will heal all the evils, fears, and displeasures of our world. I realize some days we WILL lack gratitude, and that is just how life goes. Please do not misunderstand me when I explain looking for blessings during hard times. I am not pitching a "Pollyanna" kind of attitude of all smiles. But, I do think that if we seek to see our circumstances as God sees them we will understand things much better. I do think that our genuine understanding, appreciation, and focus will help our vision of our world change for the better. It is not what we have but our attitude toward what we have at times that will set our overall perspective.

All of this in mind, blessings are not an unknown factor of life. This devotional is not to tell you anything you do not know. In fact, what you do not know, I probably do not know either. I am on the same journey in faith as each of you reading this book. This devotional is to let you discover all of the things you know and do not realize their magnitude. This devotional is to help knock the draining mentality of the world's influence and distractions. This devotional is to help you realize all that you are missing in your life. You are missing these blessings because you know such simple facts and choose to not take acknowledgement them.

DAY THREE:

Life is hard. Okay, that is a fact that none of us can hesitate to acknowledge as true. Often life may leave us broken, lost, unsatisfied, and overwhelmed. Sometimes this is from our own doing while other times we have no control. Some days we feel as though our feet never hit the ground; while other days we feel left alone with no where to go. Sometimes we wish we could have some extra "me time;" while other times we wish we could spend another day with someone we lost.

Our current society is in a constant on-the-go lifestyle. We are often found running from one activity to another. We loose sight of the full picture of life and are only consumed by the minute details. Life is full of wonders; we just forget to look for them.

> *"Blessed is she [he] who has believed that the Lord would fulfill his promises to her [him]"* (Luke 1:45 NIV).

So much of our focus has spiraled into a toxic vision. Our world is constantly distracted by countless activities causing a blur in the true purpose of our very existence.

So where are the blessings in our life? Where are the things that persuade us to keep moving? They must be somewhere or why would we all still be doing what we do? Why would there be more than seven billion people on this earth? Clearly there is something we are missing. God has placed so many things throughout our lives to fill us and bring joy unto us. We are given gifts, talents, teachings, and life so abundantly. It is time for us to recognize these things as blessings. We do not deserve a single thing. In fact, we are not deserving of even life itself. This did not stop God from giving us life and far more.

We expect life to be easy and happy. We expect everything to be like a happy children's movie all the time. When this is not the case we get angry. We feel as though life is so unfair to us. It is true life is unfair, but unfair because our God blessed us even within all our failures. If life were fair, we would not have so many of the things that we have. If life were fair, we would be facing justice for the many ways that we fall short. Our blessings flow abundantly. They come everyday in both big and little ways. Some blessings are obvious and some we must look for. Where are blessings in our life? They surround us. They hold us. They strengthen us. Our blessings are far greater than we ever account for them to be. It is time that we get out of this sour attitude of everything being miserable and simply take delight in the few or many things that are not miserable. It is time that we step down from the pedestal that we somewhere along the way placed ourselves on and realize that we deserve nothing; we have earned nothing; that blessings only come our way because we are the product of a truly loving and giving God.

In the verse from Luke above, it is revealed that we are blessed when we believe in the Lord's promises. Yes, the Lord has promised much. And the Lord does come through with all of his promises. But, none of these promises are a result of our actions. None of these promises are a result of our worth. In fact the only actions that we take that truly deserve the Lord's promises is the action of giving it all over to God. The only worth that we have that deserves the Lord's promises is the worth that we have as a child of God. We have a worth because we are a creation of God, not because of anything we have done or earned on our own. To fully understand the extent of our blessedness, we must fully understand the extent to which we do not deserve. To fully understand the extent of our blessedness, we must fully understand the vastness of the Lord's promises.

## DAY FOUR:

Now I think we can agree, we understand blessings. How can our blessings change the way we see the world though? Are we able to truly change from these "glass half empty" people the world has crushed us into? Can simply recognizing blessings cause our vision of the world to become brighter? I am not a trained psychologist, so I honestly cannot answer that question for anyone. I am also not a highly educated theologian, so I cannot tell you the magic trick (which I do not think there is one) to becoming a happier and more grateful Christian.

I do however know that there are certain powers we give to certain things. God has given us many blessings both physically and spiritually. It is important to try and change focus, giving power to these blessings. The world, however, has this ability to rob us of such things at times. When we give the world control of our emotions, it can suck us into a depression due the theft of our idea of happiness. It is important not to tie our happiness to things. Even some of our blessings can become idols and then burdens unto our souls. If we put too much power into something, it can crush us no matter what it is. Our power must lie only in our God. The worldly blessings, however nice, are only temporary. Our God gives us many blessings, and it is vital to trust his divine plan.

God may take things away from us as he sees they are no longer bringing good to us. Sometimes we idolize these things or sometimes these things are harming us and we do not notice it. We must remain faithful that God knows what is best for us. There are other things however, that God gave to us to have eternally. He blessed us with such things or abilities in order to bring lasting blessings unto us. These are the ones I want to focus on in this devotional. During the beatitudes in the book of Matthew, Jesus listed those who are blessed. Many of these blessings are things we do not recognize as blessings normally. We do not take into note that Jesus, himself, listed these blessings for his people to know. He names those who will be blessed. Until we become like the people described in the beatitudes, our blessings will be limited. We have the full ability, with Christ's help, to shape our lives in accordance. It is not easy. The world seems to do anything it can to sway us away from these blessings. The attitudes developed from the world rob us of the ability to bask in these blessings. We need to try our best to take note of the beatitudes in our life. We need to shape our life around the beatitudes. We need to understand the importance of each beatitude. We need to take knowledge and minimize the world's effect on our blessings given to us by Christ.

## DAY FIVE:

As we venture through this devotional together, there are three components involved. First, there are the devotional readings. These devotions are geared to developing different outlooks and scriptural understandings of the blessings God has given us. That with placing the power in the right hands, the world is unable to rob us of such when we do so. Next, there are challenges each day. With these challenges you are stepping out and applying your readings or searching for blessings each day. Take note on the tremendous effect such a little action can have when it is viewed as a blessing. Use these challenges to actually encourage yourself to get out of the everyday routine and maybe even out of your comfort zone. The final element is a little different. I strongly encourage you to keep what I call a "Blessing Journal." This is an outside exercise from the actual devotional challenge. This journal will be a difficult task to get in the habit of keeping. But I believe, if you get committed to it, you can possibly change your whole outlook on life. This is

11

something I started when I was going through a tough time my sophomore year. It was not as complex when I first started, but I worked out the kinks. When I was going through my rough patch, I began writing anything I had to be thankful for in my life in an old notebook. Quickly, I started to see how ridiculous my sadness was at times. This journal is different, as I do not want you to have to be in a complete depressed setting to write; I want you to get into the habit of recognizing these blessings as a way to avoid falling into the glums. I know this is not a cure all affect and some days will be better than others, but it is an experiment I want us all to journey on together.

Beginning your Blessing Journal:

The Blessing Journal is all geared to create a more optimistic outlook on your life. People say you just need to look at the silver lining, but that is much easier said than done. This idea takes that concept a bit farther. I will make a list of steps because lists are fun and easy to understand!

1. **Find a journal you won't misplace.** Maybe use this as an excuse to take a shopping trip (stores like TJ Maxx usually have ton of cute ones in their stationary section for like $5-$10 and other bookstores or office supply sections have them). I always find that the more I like and appreciate the journal the more likely I am to use it. Or if your house is like mine, you can usually find tons of old notebooks around the house and then you can reuse, reduce, and recycle! There are many ways to get a hold of a journal, notebook, or just paper, so go out and get your product.

2. **Pick a day to commit to starting the challenge.** Maybe choose a day when you have a lot of free time in the evening or a day you know you are stressed and it can help change that stress into a blessing. Whatever works best for you. Just be sure you find a time to declare a start and stick to it.

3. **Start journaling!** You will need to include the date (so you may look back on it) and at least one way you were blessed that day. This blessing can be ANYTHING at all. From spending time with family to getting a good parking space. Blessings come in all shapes and sizes and are equally important. Your writing's length is up to you. Some days they may vary. Anywhere from one sentence to a whole page, whatever you need to write about the blessings in your day works.
   ***Note- try to journal at the end of your day to end the day on a positive note no matter how good, bad, or mundane it was***

4. **Challenge yourself to keep accountable** with your journaling each day no matter how bad or good it was. I promise you that you can find some way you were blessed even on your worse days. Maybe even get friends involved too so you can create an accountability system.

5. **Track your progress**. Every so often take time to see how this challenge is impacting your view of life. Are you becoming more optimistic with faith in God? Are you noticing a little good in each day? Maybe even spin this challenge and work on your personal devotionals or quite time with God. Who knows, maybe you will even get to share this devotion and witness to others like you never dreamed possible!

The journal will not change your outlook completely. That is only something in God's capability. You need to prepare for those days that will be hard find a blessing. Not every day will be easy, but I really encourage you to keep as consistent as possible. Maybe some days you will have more to write about than others. That is okay. It is okay to only have a sentence some days and pages others. That is kind of how life works. Continue to search for blessings. I promise that the more you do this the easier it will be. Soon you will be able to recognize the little blessings without even spending much thought on it.

Our society is so fast paced and continuous that it is easy to get into a cycle, normality, a routine, and by this we get lost in the world. It is important to take time out and remember to not get so indulged in worldly manners and to recall what is important. We must take time for ourselves daily. We must separate from the world and fill our soul with truth. We must focus on the positivity in our world. Even when it is small, there are small glimpses daily. We must seize these moments and bask in the true glory of them. This journal is separate from the actual devotional. It does not have to be biblical at all. This journal is simply an amazing mean of forcing our brain to wrap around the blessings daily and turn our blinders toward these blessings and no longer away from them as the world tends to influence on us.

## Chapter 1: Open Discussion Questions

1.  What is something that has changed you from who you thought you would have been five to ten years ago?
2.  What is your reaction to lack of control at times?
3.  How can you be happy when you are having a bad day, month, or year?
4.  How close is God when you are happy versus unhappy?
5.  What is your view on your personal worth versus your worth in God?
6.  Do you know who you are? Have you accepted who you are?
7.  Where is your identity and how does this reflect on your happiness?
8.  When has a disappointment or failure led to a blessing?
9.  How do you expect God to answer your prayers? How does God actually answer your prayers?
10. How do you evaluate your blessings? Do you take daily gratitude of your blessings even on good or bad days?

## Chapter 2

# Picture Perfect

DAY ONE:

Our brain works in an interesting way. One way in particular, is our connection to words and images. When a word is read or spoken, our brain has the ability to connect it to a certain image. We each picture things differently though. Not one person's image of something is usually the exact same as another's. We all have different experiences and emotions attached to certain words. For this reason we all experience images in our own unique way. The images of our lives are constantly evolving as well. The way in which we can capture images has changed a great deal within the past fifteen years. Used to when you wanted to take a picture you had to put film in the camera, take the picture, and get the film developed. This long and expensive process limited the amount of pictures we could take. Today, we have the ability to take a picture at any time. We do not even need a camera to take pictures today. We are able to take a picture in seconds using our phones. One teenager probably takes more pictures in one day than their parents did in over a month maybe even a year when they were younger. We are so accustomed to images in our everyday lives. We all understand that images are beyond simply what we see. An image captures only so much. It is from our knowledge of this image that we are able to understand the emotions, actions, and realness of any image. With our imagination, images go beyond sight.

Throughout history, people have honored certain things through creating something in its image. There are memorials and monuments, such as the Lincoln Memorial, that have been created in an image to honor someone. Ships have figureheads dedicating the ship in honor of someone. Some military airplanes have what are called nose art that honored someone or a fictitious being. The Native Americans created mounds and totem poles in honor of gods, events, and important tribe members. The ancient Egyptians created pyramids and tombs in honor of treasures, gods, and past rulers. The ancient Romans and Greeks created statues in the image of their idols and gods. If you have not caught on by now, creating in the image or honor of someone or something has been a reoccurring action in our world. It shows a lasting respect, honor, and affection toward what it is representing.

> *"Then God said, 'Let us make mankind in our image, in our likeness, so that they may rule over the fish in the sea and the birds in the sky, over the livestock and all the wild animals, and over all creatures that move along the ground" (Genesis 1:26 NIV).*

As Christians, we grow up hearing constantly of being created in the image of God. Do we ever understand the vast honor this truly is? God, himself, desired for us to be made in his image. We were made in God's likeness. Our being was created in the image of God. This has always been one thing about Christianity that floors me in sheer amazement.

In ancient religions, they searched for an image to represent their god. This act reflected the weakness in their faith itself. They needed something tangible to lessen the distance they felt from their god. Thus, the idols they created in the image of their gods reflected a lack of their faith. They were searching for something to use as the image of their god. In contrast our God created us in the image of him. This can be confusing. We are not God? How are we the image of him? And how does this work considering we all look different? Entire denominations of Christianity have been split over this exact debate. Entire books can be written over exactly what this image is, but the truth of the matter will not be definite until we see God in heaven ourselves. The one thing that is sure is this reflection reveals the importance and divinity of our being.

We have the blessing of being made in the image of God. Our faith is not bound by searching for a tangible item to represent God. Our God can be found in his image within us. We are the tangible reflection of the God we worship. Not only do we have the blessing of finding glimpses of God within ourselves, we have the blessing of finding glimpses of God through other people. When we see a newborn letting out its first cry, we see the amazingness of our Christ's creation. When we see another person selflessly help others, we see Christ's work being done here on earth. When we see an elderly person who has lived out their life and is facing death with peace, we see Christ's promise of an afterlife being revealed through this contentment. God made us in the image of himself. How awesome is that! Often we hear people question where is our God, or what does our God look like? I know that many people who have not had an intimate relationship with their Lord feel that God is sitting up in heaven looking down on us. But, that is not how my God is. My God created human beings to reflect his image. It might not be an image as we typically think of image. We are not a "selfie" of God. But, we do reflect the essence of God. Our spirit reflects what his spirit encompasses. And the closer we walk with the Lord, the more others will see him shining through us. The more close we walk with the Lord the more we will see him in those around us.

Challenge: Look for perfection within the brokenness around. Look for the essence of God in the world around you, and understand the blessing of a God that loves us so much that he leaves the fingerprint of his image inside of us.

Memory Verse: *"Then God said, 'Let us make mankind in our image, in our likeness…'"* Genesis 1:26

### DAY TWO:

So much of our emotions are seeking out love. We search for love. We wish to love. We desire to feel loved. We have the ability to view the world in two ways. Hate or love. We can look around see all the evils of this world: the players, the haters, the heartbreakers, the fakers, the liars, and the cheats. We can focus on the corrupt and harm of the world and see all the hate around. We also have the ability to look around and see all the love in the world: the teachers, the marriages, the children playing, the first kisses, the compassionate hug, and the volunteers for those in need. We can focus on all the care being shared amongst each person and see all the love in the world. It is easy for us to get caught up in the world and lose sight of the love around. We can even lose sight of the love given to us. We get wound up and lose sight of the love we have in our life. As we lose sight of the love, we lose sight of the desire of relationships. It is hard to build relationships when we struggle to see the love surrounding them. It is hard to stay hopeful when you feel like you are unwanted. It is hard to stay in connection when you feel as though no one knows who you really are. We build masks and we hide. We hide from the world because we are scared of being denied, being vulnerable, being unwanted.

Seven billion people. There are more than seven billion people in the world. With this number in mind, it is easy to become fearful of our worth and importance. We start to think our very existence does not matter. We start to believe our actions have little purpose. We get lost in a sea of people. It is as though we are just a small midst within the world around us. We get so caught up in our small spot on the earth that at times it can feel like we are simply an ant within a large ant hill that God is looking down on. Sure, he is watching us, but can he really distinguish our very place within the mass of chaos.

> *"But I show you whom you should fear: Fear him who, after your body has been killed, has authority to throw you into hell. Yes, I tell you, fear him. Are not five sparrows sold for two pennies? Yet not one of them is forgotten by God. Indeed, the very hairs of your head are all numbered. Don't be afraid; you are worth more than many sparrows" (Luke 12:5-7 NIV).*

Our relationship with God is far more unique than any other relationship we experience. God knows us deep into our very core. He knows each of our plans and is the only person who understands our true role in the world. In times of chaos, it is easy for us to believe that we are forgotten by our God. In times of hardship, it is easy for us to be timid and think that God does not have time for us.

We are so worried about our worth and acceptance in the world. We believe we are so small in comparison to the rest of the world that our worth and love is limited. All of these apprehensions are

21

rooted in fear brought on by our world. In Luke 12:5, it is stated how ridiculous these fears are. We fear something that has limited control over us. We seek love out of something that can only love us for a brief period of time. Our fear and our acceptance should only be found in God. God is the one whom has the complete control over our entire lives. Our God is the one who designed our fate. Our love should be entrusted to him.

The passage in Luke continues to discuss the worldly value verses God's value. They state that five sparrows are sold for only two pennies. This means that one sparrow is not worth even a cent in the world's eyes. This is how we begin to feel when we view ourselves amongst the seven billion other people in the world. We feel small and our being not of importance to the rest of the world. The verse continues on to explain the worth of the Sparrows in God's eyes. Where the world seems to view the sparrow of little importance, God does not. God does not forget even ONE of them. Think of all your pennies you may have in your ashtray in your car. If one of those went missing would you even take notice? Not usually, and if you did you probably would not care enough to remember after the realization. The sparrow holds worldly worth of about less than half that of a penny. Just as we do, the world probably would simply shrug its shoulders at the realization of a sparrow gone missing, if they gave it any thought at all. Yet God remembers each sparrow. This should show us the impact our life holds in God's eyes even within the midst of the huge world we live in. Not ONE sparrow was forgotten.

God knows each hair on our head. They are each numbered and accounted for. For our existence to seem so small in our minds, this is a huge detail for our God to know about us. We forget so often that not only does our God know us; he knows everything about us. He knows every little crease on our hand. He knows every little freckle or scar on our skin. He knows every little color in our eyes. He even knows every hair on our head. I do not know about you, but if I even tried to count my hairs on my head I would either give up or lose count and focus. My God however, he knows and remembers. It was not just something he did in his free time when he was bored. He knows it out of his love for me. He knows it out of his love for you. He continues to keep connected and desires to stay in a relationship with me purely out of his love. He desires to remain knowledgeable about my every entity because of his love for me. We so easily cut this blessing short. We so easily doubt the extent of our purpose on this earth. We feel unwanted or unloved. We search for love and purpose when all along it is surrounding us and is a part of us. Our entire image and placement on earth reflects the love our savior has in store for us. We need to simply quit selling this short. He ends this verse on the most important factor. "Don't be afraid; you are worth more than many sparrows." We doubt and become fearful of our existence being a waste or unneeded. Here God is saying that our existence is worth more than many sparrows. God found each sparrow worthy of remembrance, and he finds us even more so. God desires for us to realize how important our very existence is to him. He created us in his image and created us in his love. He seeks us and desires for us to seek him. He created purpose for each of us and wishes for our acknowledgment of such.

Challenge: Reach out and remind others of their worth and purpose on this earth. It is easy for us to feel overwhelmed and small, and we must help shake that out of our minds as we are loved and held with a great amount of worth.

Memory Verse: *"Indeed the very hairs of your head are all numbered. Don't be afraid; you are worth more than many sparrow."* Luke 12:7

## DAY THREE:

Any one who has attempted to study anatomy and any part of the human body realizes the intricacy and complexity of the human body. We are created with many different systems and organs and functions of each. Our body works together so smoothly to make our lives work in the ways they are shaped to. Not one body part works separately. Your leg cannot work without the bones shifting correctly, the muscles contracting, the brain instructing the action, and each part in between. Often we do not realize the wonders of our own body. On most days everything functions correctly and not one thought goes into our bodies doing all the work they do.

At times our bodies do not do their jobs correctly, and this is when our eyes open to the true glory of each piece. For example, as a child grows up they eat and drink and do not usually put any thought into what they eat and the impact it has. That is how I was growing up at least. You gave me food, and I was more than happy to eat it no problem. Then in 2008, that changed. I started to thirst constantly, nap any chance I got, had little energy to do much of anything, and then the final red flag approached when in two weeks I had lost about twenty-five pounds. I went from weighing about eighty pounds as an eleven year old to weighing almost fifty. To say I was skin and bones was no exaggeration at all. I went to the doctor multiple times to try and figure out the cause to all these changes. Finally on the third visit they took blood and sent me to Scottish Rite Hospital. I was diagnosed with type-one diabetes. For those who do not know, this is an autoimmune disease in which the body destroys all of its beta cells. Without the beta cells in the body, you are unable to produce insulin, which is needed to break down sugar within the blood. This is a disease that has no cure. As an eleven year old I had to learn to accept my body with this complication and learn how to compensate by giving shots and carefully counting my food intake. This was when my eyes were first opened to the complexity of the body and the blessing our health really is.

*"For you created my inmost being; you knit me together in my mother's womb. I praise you because I am fearfully and wonderfully made; your works are wonderful, I know that full well" (Psalm 139:13-14 NIV).*

The human body is probably one of the greatest testimonies to the complexity of creation. One organ in itself is a miracle. The fact that each of these organs work together to sustain the life of the human body is without a doubt a miracle. In addition to the amazing physical activities of the body, the complexity of psychology and emotions have a great effect on the body's process as well. Our bodies are just a miracle in all the ways God created them to work.

People look into mirrors several times throughout the day. Each time one looks into the mirror they tend to search for what needs to be fixed. Is their hair in order, are their teeth clean, do they have blemishes that need covering, is there excess fat that they should lose, and are there new wrinkles they have developed? We look into a mirror and often see all the imperfections present. We pick and prod at ourselves trying to decide what to do to make our image look better. We so easily lose sight of all the blessings that are wrapped into the image we view each time we look into the mirror. In fact, the simple action of looking into the mirror is a blessing in itself, as we must have functioning eyes to do so. We definitely are wonderfully made, yet we take this for granted more often than not.

A loving God designed the physiology of our body in a similar fashion as an architect designs a building. He designed it in a manner that we above all other living beings are able to live out our lives sustainably and think, reason, and learn from past experiences. In a sense, next to salvation, the greatest gift God has and can ever give us is ourselves and who he made us to be. Even though at times our bodies may have diseases, our God uses those times of hardship for a greater story. It might be revealing the blessings present in a new vision, drawing us closer to him, or giving us an experience to minister through; no matter the case it does not drain from the way in which our bodies were wonderfully made. The view we see our bodies through is quite different from the view God sees his creation. God created us perfectly in his eyes. We are his masterpieces. We are his love. We are his legacy. Our view of ourselves is so different because so often we view our bodies as just our bodies. We leave out the thought of our bodies being a wonderful part of God's creation. We do not acknowledge the fact that God created each of us the way he did for his purpose. It is easy for us to view ourselves through the lens of the world. The world points to all our flaws and mistakes. We really need to work our hardest to view ourselves through the lens of our God. God views us with love, admiration, and purpose. When we learn to look at ourselves through God's eyes and not our eyes, our self-worth, self-esteem, and blessings should increase dramatically.

---

Challenge: Take a "selfie" and reflect on your view of yourself verses God's view. If you struggle with self-esteem maybe write a list of all the blessings and goodness God created in you and place this in your bathroom on your mirror, so you may have a constant reminder to change your view of yourself from the world's to your God's view.

Memory Verse: "*Your works are wonderful, I know that full well.*" Psalm 139:14

---

## DAY FOUR:

I am a common girl. There is absolutely no denying it. If you know me, you know it is very true. One factor that I exceed in, as a girl, is the amount of time it takes me to get ready. Now I do have to make one comment on this, it is not the getting ready as much so as all the decisions that go into getting ready. I would say on average, it takes me about three to four attempts to pick an outfit to wear each day. I mean it is a tough decision. I will have to commit to this outfit for an entire day or most of the day at least. What if I meet someone famous? What if I have to get my picture made? What if I run across my soul mate? I need to look good in case any of these things may happen. I mean if I do not look my best then I might as well look my worst. Again, okay, I am a common girl. Another factor on this note, random side fact, my room would be super clean if this were not the case. If you go into my room, before I have the chance to stop you, you will find mounds of outfits that got rejected all over my floor. Decisions are hard, okay!

This indecisiveness is not just within my getting ready process of my day. It seems as though this is a nature I carry throughout much of the day. When I wake up and am out the door more decisions lie ahead. What do I want to eat? That is a very hard one, as I generally love food. It is another one of those extremely important decisions that once you commit, you commit. Then along side with what should I eat, there is always the decision of the drink to wash it down. To be honest, I really only drink water and coffee. Every once in a while, I may mix it up, but that is a rare decision. Continuing throughout my day there are other things that are hard to decide upon. What homework is most important? Do I have time to hang out with friends? Should I have studied more for that test? We all usually spend so much time with our brains spinning in circles trying to wrap ourselves around all of these questions that lay upon our hearts. Sometimes we spend so much of our time worrying about every little thing, that when there is nothing to worry about, we worry about not worrying. OH MY. That was a lot of worrying within one single sentence. It is honestly true. The world we are currently in seems to be so accustomed to worrying that it is almost a default. It feels out of the ordinary for us to not be worrying.

> *"'Therefore I tell you, do not worry about your life, what you will eat or drink; or about your body, what you will wear. Is not life more than food, and the body more than clothes? Look at the birds of the air; they do not sow or reap or store away in barns, and yet your heavenly Father feeds them. Are you not more valuable than they? Can any of you by worrying add a single hour to your life?'" (Matthew 6:25-27 NIV).*

Our human desire of keeping up with the rest of the world brings much anxiety. We try to do so much all at once and all on our own. We try to stay strong and keep everything perfect. The world we live in emphasizes for each of us to be accountable for ourselves. We are told we need to do better, reach above the rest, and to constantly be improving. Many of us get caught up in trying to measure up to the world's unobtainable standards. We get worn down and are left in a constant state of anxiety trying to match up to the world on our own. Thank goodness this is not what our God seeks for us. We cling to our own works. We need to recognize the faithfulness of God and trust God not ourselves. We believe as though we can accomplish it all on our own, yet we get run down and our fear haunts us each step along the way.

We are blessed with a God that loves us dearly to provide the way. Not only did he create us in such a perfect way but also he provided our path to journey along during our lifetime. He provides the way. The world teaches us that if we want to achieve greatness we must work at it. We forget that some things are out of our hands. We forget that some things we must have faith in God's assurance that they will work out in our benefit. We waste so much of our time worrying about every aspect of our lives. We spend so much of our time struggling to accept reality as it is. We have gotten to a point that we even worry when God has us in his hands and everything is fine, simply because this lack of control and chaos is odd for us. Faith is truly odd and hard for us to accept in this society. Faith in God to provide is so odd since we are so used to having to do it all on our own.

> *"God did this so that they would seek him and perhaps reach out for him and find him, though he is not far from any one of us. For in him we live and move and have our being. As some of your own poets have said, We are his offspring" (Acts 17:27-28 NIV).*

Paul's words in this passage of Acts bring peace to all of my anxieties. Anxiety has been an issue that is hard for me to cope with during my faith journey. It is so hard for me to let go of the control and fear allowing God to take control. Sometimes I do not even notice when my anxieties creep up, but when they do they have the ability to take over all my emotions.

In this passage, I am reminded of one of the reasons I believe God allowed for many others and

31

myself to struggle with anxiety. With my anxiety, I must seek and reach out to God. I am forced to break down all walls of control and let go to God during panic attacks. It takes my mind to be surround by anxiety for it to realize its need to step away, to let go, to give it to God. Once my mind allows itself to step away, I am then able to experience God in his fullness. He takes my life into his hands once again and restores my faith. He takes away each worry and forces me to trust. He reminds me of all his plans for my future and the strength he will continue to give me along the way. The overthinking, stubborn person, I am, refuses to let go until letting go is all they can possibly do.

God has blessed us each with his care. He prepares the way for us. Unlike the world, our God does not wish for us to do it on our own. Unlike the world, our God sets our path and provides for us. He wishes for us to remain completely faithful and not to doubt. He wishes for us to abandon all anxieties at the door and allow for him to overwhelm us with his close faithfulness. We are his offspring. He sees worth, purpose, and love in us. Each of us were created and loved uniquely. He promises not to abandon us. He promises not to leave us thirsty, hungry, or ragged. His love and faithfulness is far greater than anything the world could possibly provide, and the anxiety the world causes wastes our time and exhaust our soul.

Challenge: Go on a hike or nature walk and enjoy God's creation and all the wonderful ways he provides for each part of it.

Memory Verse: "*Can any of you by worrying add a single hour to your life?*" Matthew 6:27

## DAY FIVE:

The creation is by far one of the greatest blessings we have been given. I mean, it is who we are, how God created us, how we respond, how we work, and how we live. The way in which God created the world is amazing, but the way in which he created us far surpasses that. God created us to be complex beings. One of these complexities is the way in which God has blessed us with instincts and intuitions that allow for our bodies to stay in good health.

It is easy for us to get caught up in the world. We get in a rush and get caught up in the madness. Without these instincts and intuitions, we could possibly abandon our body's needs. With these instincts and intuitions, we are able to stay on a course that maintains health and is fundamental toward thriving in life. When we are getting sleepy and getting tired, we yawn and nod off. It takes every ounce of energy to keep our eyes open. Now most people, like myself, would never sleep more than a few hours a day, or just sleep all day then not sleep for days. Our bodies need sleep and our bodies have these instincts that are triggered to persuade us to get to sleep when we are tired.

Another instinct at hand is for our moral health. When we are doing something that we are not supposed to be doing we get this discomfort in our gut, the "uh oh feeling." At first we might think this is something that we learn and is not biological, but if we truly reflect on this, every time we consider something we know we should not do our heart rate increases and the hairs on our neck stand up. Some people begin to develop ticks such as the twitching of the eye or the jumpiness of their actions. In fact, our law enforcement uses these instincts to develop lie-detecting tests. It is amazing the built in intuition that God has given us to direct our bodies in the route of good not harm.

We all know that embarrassing moment, the room is quiet and without the ability to stop this embarrassment, our stomach lets out a loud grumble. Our body has extraordinary means of informing us that it is hungry. Some of the weird people, like me, even try "shh"ing it to get it to cut it out, as it is not the right time or place to be reminded of our hunger. Our body knows when it needs to be filled with food in order to continue on the energy and nourishment it has or needs. The body is not shy with informing us of this matter as well. We become so discomforted that if we continue to ignore such hunger would be more of a hassle than simply giving in and feeding it. Along side with the hunger is its friend, thirst. Thirst has a harsh and much quieter form of screaming out for attention. Generally it is simply by the dryness of the throat and weakness of the body. If we ignore it for too long, and such thirst develops into dehydration, worst screams can become such as headaches, vomiting, fainting, and clamminess. Our health is put in danger when we ignore the screams of hunger or thirst. Our body knows what it needs to be healthy and God created it to do all it can to prevent us from ignoring its basic needs.

> *"Blessed are those who hunger and thirst for righteousness, for they will be filled" (Matthew 5:6 NIV).*

Our bodies recognize hunger and thirst very clearly. Aside from the biological sense of hunger and thirst, our bodies recognize our spiritual hunger and thirst. We are created to seek and need God for our wellbeing. Many of us get caught up in the world and begin to ignore this need. There are three general reasons we do this. One is simply we are busy. We have a lot going on in our lives and we just do not have the time it takes to pray, read God's word, or go to Church. We think we must live our lives first before we can worship the one whom gave us this life. Another reason is when we are simply having too much fun. We are enjoying our life going to parties, getting black out drunk, and doing adventurous rebellions with our friends. Sure, some of these may be against our beliefs and against our moral compass, but it is fun and no one wants to be a party pooper. And the final reason, we get so low and down and feel as though there is no point in reaching out and trying. We feel as though our being does not matter and so why should we try to seek out God. Yet, as we replace this need for God in our soul with worldly substitutes, our body knows it is not filled. It continues to fill empty and fall deeper. We cry out, as we desire more. We feed more and more into these worldly matters and are still left unsatisfied.

Our God created our being so complex that even when we ignore our spiritual need, our body will not. Our body will continue to cry for more and search in other areas. This beatitude addresses the fact that until we only hunger and thirst for righteousness from God, we will not be filled. Those who have accepted their body's need for righteousness are those that are filled. Just as in a bulimic person may eat enough food to fill their body but will turn around and bring it back up. This is how we treat our body when we try to satisfy it with worldly things. We may fill it just enough to get rid of the aching of the hunger, but it is only temporary and before we know it, we have vomited out the filling and are left empty once again. The only way we are blessed with fulfillment is when we stop ignoring and substituting our body's hunger and thirst for righteousness. God blessed us creating our body in a way that it wants his presence. He created us to live in his arms. He created us to do great things. We must turn away from the world that presses on us to ignore this instinct and intuition that was created within us, and we must seek it and tend to it to allow our soul to be filled.

Challenge: Watch the sunset or sunrise. Take note of the complexity of the world, and God's purpose with each element it holds.

Memory Verse: *"Blessed are those who hunger and thirst for righteousness, for they will be filled."* Matthew 5:6

## Chapter 2: Open Discussion Questions

1. What does it mean to be in the image of something?
2. In taking a picture, how does this capture the image you are seeing versus the image that is kept?
3. What does the image have to do with love?
4. Do you feel the love of God within your creation?
5. How does understanding your worth help you grow in faith?
6. Does your worth lie in God or the world?
7. How does God care for his creation?
8. Do you trust God as much as you worry about your being?
9. What does it mean to be a child of God?
10. What is your importance in this world?

## Chapter 3

# Throwback

DAY ONE:

God created us to grow up and mature along the journey. As a newborn, you are completely dependent on your parents to supply all your needs and to tend to you. Soon you begin to walk, talk, and make decisions on your own. Aside from the physical growing, you mentally grow and mature along the way. You become curious and get into things you maybe should not. You learn lessons the hard way after shocking yourself by sticking that paperclip in the outlet. You start dreaming. One day you might want to be the president but soon you grow up and chose a job for which you have a niche. You grew up thinking boys and girls had cooties and later will do any and everything to get to see that special someone.

Childlike innocence and wonder is a beautiful part of our lives. It does not end after you are older. You are constantly surrounded by the innocence and wonder from children of all ages. When I was younger I always followed the older crowd. I had two older brothers, so I wanted to hang out with their group of friends. I then started developing many role models along the way. I looked up to these older kids, and wanted to be just like them. As I got older the tables have turned. One of the most fulfilling blessings God has given me in my life, personally, is the chance to be a mentor for young kids just as I had when I was there age. Being able to give advice and help these younger kids as they progress through this chaotic life brings so much joy to my life in return. Once you have grown up, it then becomes your turn to help assist the young ones as they venture on their maturing journey.

What if that is not the complete case? I am here to say enough with growing up. Let us all run away to "Neverland" and never come back. What if this "Real World" that we hear about so often does not even exist? It is ridiculous that growing up involves so much loss. Loss of innocence, dreams, trust, and wonder. God did not give us the sense of wonder and innocence just for the short time of our youth.

> *"He called a little child to him and placed the child among them. And he said: 'Truly I tell you, unless you change and become like little children, you will never enter the kingdom of heaven. Therefore, whoever takes the lowly position of this child is the greatest in the kingdom of heaven'"* *(Matthew 18:2-4 NIV).*

This verse shows truly just how important our childlike nature is to God. When Jesus used a child to teach the importance of innocence when entering the kingdom of heaven, I am sure he really shook up his students. Just as many times throughout scripture, the disciples came to Jesus asking a question that they thought they already knew the answer. Jesus never lets them win that easily. The disciples come to Jesus in Matthew 17 asking who is the greatest in the kingdom of heaven. This is a group of followers who have devoted their lives to Jesus' ministry and seek his approval daily. Surely, Christ would reassure them that they have done well and will be great in heaven, right? Not quite the case. Jesus turns to a child as an example. He does not say they must view life like a child, or act like a child. He tells them they must CHANGE and BECOME like little children. And this command is not to be great in the kingdom of heaven, no, this is to simply enter the kingdom of heaven. WOW. That seems bold. We spend all this time growing up only to be told to change like little children?

We must open our callous heart. When much of this world breaks us down we are almost forced to abandon our childlikeness to grow. I know when I talk to children that have such hope and brightness still intact, I get upset and angry at the world. Often I find myself reminiscing about the "old me." It seems as though the person I was just four years ago is an entirely different person than who I am today. The world has the ability to wear us down, decay our hope, and dim our light. It is not a simple task. As we are trying to live our life to become better people and more Christ like, we are found reading scripture daily, praying daily, ministering, and meditating. All these actions seem to be pulling us away from childlike behaviors. These actions are great, maturing, and building in wisdom. A child does not seem to take such serious actions. A child dreams, plays, adventures, and hopes. This is one of the ironies in the message Christ came to deliver.

We must open our callous hearts to God and all his wisdom. Just as I once stated, we are blessed in the ability to help younger kids along their journey of life, the ultimate mentor we are blessed with is Christ. We must be able to step away from all that this world has taught us, and come to him with childlike innocence and childlike trust. God will always have the upmost knowledge. He knows our entire plan. We have to step away from our stubborn maturity and allow him to show us the way. We are blessed to not be expected to grow up and know it all. We are blessed to not be expected to take on this world on our own. We are always children to God, and until we become like little children, we will never have the full openness needed to enter his kingdom. Christ does not seek to rob us of any pieces; the world does a good job of that. Christ seeks for us to cling to our innocence, dreams, trust, and wonder as children of God.

Challenge: Listen and respect a child's dreams and thoughts in order to remind yourself of the true essence God seeks for us to hold in childlike wonder.

Memory Verse: *"Truly I tell you, unless you change and become like little children, you will never enter the kingdom of heaven."* Matthew 18:2-4

## DAY TWO:

This might just be a "me" thing, since I am a sensitive and caring soul, but one of the sweetest sights is watching a mother comfort her child. We all know the scenario, the child starts wailing and pitching a fit; this could be from not getting the cookie they wanted or from falling and hitting their head. No matter what caused the child to get upset, it is now as if the child's entire world is collapsing around them. The screaming seems as though it is an ongoing anthem of the child's retaliation on whatever upset them. Next, sometimes, even within a few moments, the most magnificent change occurs. The mother comes to the child and is able to seize the war of emotions to a full halt. The cries and distraught look on the child's face can become a smile or even laughter within a few seconds. The traumatic event has come to a close and all thanks are due to the precious mother. This is an event that always brings joy to my heart. The comfort and trust of the mother in this child's time of need is such a beautiful sight.

No one knows a child as the mother does. From the minute the mother sets eyes on her child, the welfare of the child is entrusted to her. Within days, she is able to distinguish the difference between each of its cries, whines, and grunts. She learns the cry of discomfort, hunger, and pain. She is able to tell by the very expression on her child's face, what their every thought is. She is uniquely able to anticipate the needs of her child, and provide those needs. Her voice is recognized by the child from all the voices around. She has the ability to nourish the child when nourishment is needed. When the child is in pain, she does not only recognize that but feels the pain herself. It is as if the blueprint of this child's being is imprinted on her heart. For this reason, when the child enters into a situation of danger through its rebellious actions, she has the ability to determine the best course to take to guide him on the right path.

> *"'I will extend peace to her like a river, and the wealth of nations like a flooding stream; you will nurse and be carried on her arm and dandled on her knees. As a mother comforts her child, so will I comfort you; and you will be comforted over Jerusalem'"* *(Isaiah 66:12-13 NIV).*

Our childlike nature goes beyond the simple openness and actions of a child. From this passage in Isaiah, we see that God comforts us just like a mother comforts her child. So often, we get frustrated with the way in which God is handling our lives. We think he has abandoned us, does not recognize us, or even is unfair to us. We ignore the truth that God knows us just as a mother knows her child. God knows us better than we even know ourselves. He knows our every hair. He knows our every cry. He knows our every thought. He can anticipate our every need, and knows just how to provide it. He nourishes our soul when nothing else can nourish it fully, aside from him. We forget so often that when we are in pain, Christ experiences that pain along side of us. He does not wish for us to cry. His heart breaks when ours does.

The ways in which God comforts us changes based on the situation at hand, just as the mother's way to comfort depends on the source of the struggle. When a child is doing something they should not, but the mother knows it does not endanger their life, sometimes the best approach is to let the child learn the hard way. The child will continue out their rebellious actions and will learn on their own that it was not for their benefit. The child will then correlate the pain or harm done with the action and not do it again. Just as in this scenario, God may not step in just yet. He knows the best way for us to learn sometimes is from our mistakes. This does not mean God has abandoned us. This means God knows that we will only learn if we suffer the consequence ourselves. This is an amazing fact considering our God is a God who feels our pain. He knows these actions of our own might hurt us, and it will hurt him to see us get hurt, yet he knows that it is best for him to let it be so we can truly grow. Thinking of this scenario in that context shows just how polar this is from abandonment. Sometimes, when a mother sees immediate danger coming her child's way, she will step in and do anything and everything to prevent this from happening. If a child is running out to the road while a truck is speeding by, the mother is not going to simply sit back and allow the child to learn by getting hit. No, the mother is going to sprint out and pick her child up and lecture the child about running out toward the road. Sometimes, God sees that we are running toward a path of destruction away from him, and in these situations he will do anything and everything to pull us out of this danger. Sometimes we are stubborn and continue on, but this does not mean God is not going to continue putting roadblocks in our way. He loves us and wants to see us prosper, no matter what the case may be. Unfortunately, sometimes the things that hurt us are not of our own doing. Sickness, betrayal, or losses are things that are not in our control, but will hurt us just the same. These are times when the mother simply holds and comforts her child. She knows there is not much she may do to take away the pain her child holds. God can take away our pain if he so chooses. But, sometimes he realizes that we will grow from our pain. In these cases, God is the ultimate refuge for his children. God does not wish for us to carry the pain of these struggles alone. He will hold us, comfort us, and promise to use these difficult times to spring greatness later on. These are the times when it is hardest to trust in God's comfort, but it is promised countless times that comfort will come to those in need. He will extend peace like a river unto each child who is in pain and bring comfort just as a mother comforts her child.

One of the most comforting elements of the mother and child relationship is as simple as the mother's voice. The child knows the mother's voice not by sound but by the tone. A child can recognize whether it is in trouble, needed, or pleased with all by the mother's voice. For the mother's voice to play such a substantial role in the child's life there must be a close relationship. Not only are we able to have this relationship with God, it is one he desires. God wants us to know his voice and every tone associated with it. We are his children and he craves for us to recognize his voice above the confusion of the world. Sadly, this is something most Christians suffer with. We build up walls. We lack trust. We disconnect from our communication with God. His voice is hidden and ignored. We loose our childlike behavior and then loose our dependence upon his very voice. This is the driving factor to why our blessing of motherly comfort from God is cut short. We ignore his voice, comfort, and direction. When we cut off this connection with our God, we loose more than just our comfort, we loose this relationship he has created for us. Our God is not one who sits on a throne above and casts lightening bolts down on us when we wrong him! Our God is one who desires to walk with us. Our God is one who desires to talk with us. In this passage of Isaiah, it even says, "to be carried on her arm and dandled on her knees." This description brings to me an image of our God as not only comforting with love but also playful in love. Just imagine our God playing with us and dandling us on his knees. He has come down to us. There is no more intimate relationship than to picture a child on its parent's lap. This intimate relationship is one our God seeks; I can go on and on about how blessed that makes me, personally, feel. We must remain childlike and lean on God for nourishment, comfort, and joy. God is and should be our one provider of peace at all times.

Challenge: Give thanks for all the things you have the ability to do due to your youth. Go out and do them remembering all the youth you still have.

Memory Verse: "*As a mother comforts her child, so will I comfort you....*" Isaiah 66:13

## DAY THREE:

We all know what it is like to crave something. You develop this desire that only this one thing will satisfy. You will do anything to get your hands on this one thing to break this need. I myself have two cravings that creep up in my life most often. It may seem cliché, but I get cravings for either coffee or chocolate that feels as though I will go absolutely mad if I do not get them. My friends make fun of me because this craving is so intense that I really do spend more of my time at Starbucks drinking coffee or in my basement with chocolate and a movie marathon. One of my friends lost it in laughter when we were at Starbucks and noticed my phone automatically connected to their WiFi when it rarely does that at my own house.

Cravings are something many of us experience, some more than others. They come and go each day. They do not have to be food though. You are able to crave an item, an activity, or a person. Cravings are just this non-substitutable desire for something that will not leave until you fulfill it.

Cravings can be beneficial or toxic. This all determines what the item is and how far the craving will take us. The craving for a newborn to be fed by its mother is a beneficial craving. This child knows the richness and fulfillment of the mother's milk and will cry and cry until it is fed. This is vital to the newborn's health. The child is unable to simply tell the mother of its thirst, but if it went unfed it will be malnourished. The child has this nature of craving its mother's milk from birth. It is beneficial as it nourishes the child and places the non-substitutable need for their mother in their life early on. The craving of a child's sweet tooth can be detrimental. This child wants to satisfy their sweet tooth more than anything, but this is not always a healthy choice. If the child has already had a snack or if it is not the right timing for a snack, this craving can lead to an incident. They will scream and yell, throw a fit, give an attitude, all because they were unable to satisfy this craving. But, if they are given into and given this snack before they receive proper nutrition then their appetite will be weak and this nourishment would be robbed from them. If they are given this snack too close to bedtime, they will be wired and unable to sleep, thus being robbed of vital rest to be functional the next day. These same instances are present in all cravings of our lives. We want them so badly. If we are unable to achieve them, we feel as if the world will fall around us, but at times, when we do receive them, they do more harm than good.

> *"Therefore rid yourselves of all malice and all deceit, hypocrisy, envy, and slander of every kind. Like newborn babies, crave pure spiritual milk, so that by it you may grow up in your salvation, now that you have tasted that the Lord is good" (1 Peter 2:1-3 NIV).*

The metaphor of an infant craving milk is used in this passage from Peter. This brings a reminder of just how strong our need for salvation should be. We are to be childlike in our cravings for God. This is not only what we need to stay spiritually sound but also what we must crave to stay nourished. Not one day should pass without our need for God's presence and salvation in our lives just as not one day should pass without a newborn's cravings of their mother's milk. Just as newborns generally wake starving, we must crave God's presence in our lives from the very moment we open our eyes. This desire should come without second thought and we must seek it until we are filled with his love and promise throughout our lives.

This desire for God in our lives must be without substitution. Not one thing can take the place of our need for him. In fact, when we try to substitute something for this craving, it will do damage just as the child's craving of sweets. We will need more and more of this substitution as it fills the void immediately but does not fulfill our spiritual nutrition needed. God's presence and salvation is the one thing that can fill us whole and not rob us of anything. It is stated at the beginning of the passage that we must "rid [ourselves] of all malice and all deceit, hypocrisy, envy, and slander of every kind." These substitutions may satisfy an immediate desire of energy or fulfillment, but they do not nourish us fully. We truly must rid ourselves of all these substitutes for all that God has to offer. Continuing to take part in these will rob us of life. It is easy to see why a child is robbed of an appetite when they indulge in a snack without first nourishment. This same action goes for us. Until we get our nourishment from God, our life will be robbed from the true appetite of joy. Once we indulge in God's presence and salvation, our desire for these toxic replacements will soon fade. They are unneeded. They no longer satisfy our craving. They do not fill us, as we need.

Many of us go day to day seeking fulfillment. We search in every location to find this satisfaction. We scream and yell, throw a fit, give an attitude, until we satisfy this craving for more. Our world surrounds us with methods to fulfill this need, yet none have the long-term success in holding such satisfaction. We must wake each day seeking God's presence. We must not give in until we are filled with his salvation. We must not allow substitutions to take place. It is important that we hold this childlike craving for God. No other will ever satisfy, and until we allow this truth to take hold of our life, our joy will continually be robbed by this world.

Challenge: Take a younger friend or family member out for a treat. Enjoy time and grow in relationship with them. Maybe even spoil them with something they love and crave and rarely get.

Memory Verse: *"Like newborn babies, crave pure spiritual milk, so that by you may grow up in your salvation."* 1 Peter 2:2

## DAY FOUR:

My whole life I have been a person who dreams big. I remember as a child I would tell my parents the most crazy and extravagant occupations I wanted to do when I grew up. I told them I was going to be an archeologist and discover a dinosaur. I told them I was going to be a dancer in Las Vegas

51

or Broadway. I told them I was going to be the first girl President. I told them I was going to be the endocrinologist that discovered the cure to diabetes. My dreams were never small and I never allowed for anyone to tell me I could not accomplish them. Even today, I am still stubborn natured in my dreaming. If someone tells me that I am too young to do something or that idea is irrational and will never work, it gives me an even greater drive to do it and prove them wrong. I have always had this piece of my heart that believed I could accomplish anything I work hard enough to do it.

In school, I had a strong competitive edge. I wanted to learn more than anything. Even in elementary school, if a concept did not come easily to me I worked at it until I could teach it myself practically. I was never the child that just wanted to have fun. I was that child who was constantly looking for something new to get involved in and to explore. However, I was the baby in my family. Not just my immediate family, my entire family. Where I lived was unlike most children growing up. I lived next door to most all of my mom's side of the family. On one side of the road were our family and all of my mom's sibling's families. Across the road were my grandmother, two of her siblings, and their families. I was the youngest amongst all of these cousins, aunts, and uncles. I was constantly being told how I was too young to do certain things. I was constantly being told of how cute I was for my big imagination. This would drive me absolutely crazy! I was not cute. I was not young. I was just as capable as the next person to do anything and dream anything. I did not allow for this to tear me down, I used this as motivation. Whenever someone told me I was too young, the drive to prove them wrong was boosted times ten.

> *"Don't let anyone look down on you because you are young, but set an example for the believers in speech, in conduct, in love, in faith, and in purity. Until I come, devote yourself to public reading of Scripture, to preaching and to teaching. Do not neglect your gift, which was given you through prophecy when the body of elders laid their hands on you" (1 Timothy 4:12-14 NIV).*

Paul addresses this very topic in 1 Timothy 4:12-14, it is stated for the youth to set an example and for none to look down upon them. This comes into play with the childlike wonder and dreaming. You must dream and pursue God's call in your life no matter your age or experience. God will equip the unequipped. (Watch out, I will use this saying a lot because it is one of my favorites.) It is so easy to adopt the thoughts of the world that you must be qualified and old enough to do great things. God has placed gifts within all of us. These gifts when combined with the greatness of God's power have the capability to do amazing things. If we always believe that we are too young, we will continuously cut ourselves short of being used for his kingdom. It could be something as simple as handing out blankets to those in need, starting a band to inspire others with our gift in music, leading a Bible study on our own doing, or even going on a mission trip to witness to other nations. No matter what the calling or gift is; we must not ignore it due to ideals of this world.

Often it is easy to become negative and excuse this negativity as being a realist. God is far beyond our knowledge and capabilities. It is vital for us to always remain faithful to his plan and trust in him to guide us if it is in his will. In the world we live in today, this is not an easy concept. It takes a bold step to dream big. We truly look irrational when we dream so big, but have faith in God to bring it to reality. God's reality is much different from our reality. The world has a tendency to shut down dreams. We must step out and truly trust and dream, not allowing for the world to shut our dreams down as imagination and impossible.

It is easy for us to get so caught up in the "real world" and see only the flaws to come. I have experienced several ministers even who have scoffed at others or my own dreams and ideas; they simply told me good luck. The first time I experienced this I got angry. I wanted to pitch a fit because I thought the minister would be encourageing. Now I understand, this is how many of us respond to other's dreams. We do not have the same calling or vision, as God is placing on this individual. It is hard to see past the complications. We can get so wrapped up in this world that we look down upon not only the children but also any dreamer. Aside from our own dreams, it is important for us to not look down upon others. We must always dream like children and remain hopeful like children. To dream is to hold hope and faith to a whole other level. To dream is to place our trust in God to carry out this plan that is impossible in our own hands. To dream is to truly place our life in God's hands to be used for a purpose greater than us. It is one of the upmost blessings in my life. Without dreaming, the world would be so much smaller. Without dreaming, no change or progress would be possible. Without dreaming, the colors would simply fade to black and white.

Challenge: Do something you used to do when you were a child. Color, dance, play, swim, swing, build a blanket fort, eat a huge ice cream Sunday, or watch cartoons. Maybe do all at the same time. Whatever it may be, go do it and do it without shame but joy!

Memory Verse: *"Don't let anyone look down on you because you are young, but set an example for the believers in speech, in conduct, in love, in faith, and in purity." 1 Timothy 4:12*

## DAY FIVE:

I think we can all agree on what makes children so stinking adorable, their innocence. They are born into this world with light in their hearts. Their eyes that see love in everyone without judgment, their hands that cling tight to their parents as if they could keep them safe from all harm of this world, their imagination that can create a joyful surrounding no matter the circumstance, their carefree attitude without the anxieties of the world weighing down upon them; all these characteristics shape the innocence of the children in our lives. Innocence is pure and simply beautiful. We look at these children and see hope through this innocence. Their world is beautiful and clean. Their love is selfless and free. Their mind is learning and open. The children are blessed with such innocence that makes them able to see freely in this world.

We often view these children with slight envy. We strive to change our closed minds to be open and accepting again. We reminisce on our days when we lived so freely. We long for the beautiful world we used to know. We look back to when our world was filled with hope. We have emotional scars that are left behind each time we are harmed by others and begin to doubt the beautiful world around. We soon learn to look out for ourselves before the welfare of others. In fact, this is what we are taught to do. On top of this, there are anxieties we develop as we focus so much on fear and mistakes. Even when these events are unlikely to occur, we rob ourselves of the joy that could come by focusing our attention on these doubts. It is odd that we have a tendency to cling to these scars. They are the last things we seem to let go of when surrendering to God. Once we have given God our self-preservation, self-doubt, and anxieties, we begin to return to the childlike innocence and pure heartedness in God's hands.

We long for this innocence to return to us, and the funny thing is that God longs for this innocence to return as well. We never were meant to be broken down by the world. God wished for us to stay free, selfless, hopeful, and in awe of creation. Fear separated us. Judgment weighed down upon us. Pain left us weak. Pressures of the world left us filled with anxiety.

> *"Blessed are the pure in heart, for they will see God" (Matthew 5:8 NIV).*

In this Beatitude, Jesus declares those with a pure heart to be blessed. What is a pure heart? The pure hearted people are those who are selfless, hopeful, and overall most childlike with their innocence. These people see the beauty in the world around. They are the ones who do not allow the world to weigh upon their hearts. The world can cause us to become callous, narrow-minded, and doubtful. Those with a pure heart abstain from this temptation and give their trust to God. The people in our lives that seem most pure are those who have the capability to give anything pressing upon them to God. It seems as though the older we get, the harder this act becomes. The more pain and heartache we experience the harder it is to put our complete trust into God. Until we can accomplish this feat, we will never remain pure at heart. Until we separate from this world, we will never regain the innocence of our youth. Until we let go of the things of this world that we cling to, we will never walk freely with God.

Jesus declared the pure at heart to be those who will see God; at first it seems odd and even slightly unfair. We all are supposed to see God are we not? We are. The pure in heart are the ones who have the blessing of seeing God daily. Through their pureness and trust, they have the ability to draw closest to God. They have fewer things that separate them from their relationship with God. Those who are not pure in heart have their relationship with God clouded by their insecurities, fears, sins, and anxieties. When we are able to remain pure in heart, our vision of God is free from this fog of the world. When we are able to remain pure in heart, our openness allows for us to experience God's presence more clearly. This verse is difficult to understand until you accept that we see God here on earth. Those who are pure in heart have the ability to recognize God amongst us. They can pin point the moments when God is reaching down to them. They do not allow the world to tell them otherwise. They do not allow the world to place doubt amongst them. They do not allow the world to separate them from this trust.

God has blessed us with the ability to be pure and innocent even outside of our youth. He desires us to remain clean from the world and in relationship with him. It is very difficult to hold true to this blessing as the world presses down so harshly on us. Once we are able to separate our heart from this world, we will experience God like never before. Once we are able to remain pure, we will see God daily and our relationship will be the closer than ever.

Challenge: Dream big and wildly like a child. Jot some of these thoughts down and place them in a location you will see often. Remember to keep your heart pure from the world and close to God. Only allow God to tell you where you stand amongst the kingdom.

Memory Verse: *"Blessed are the pure in heart, for they will see God."* Matthew 5:8

## Chapter 3: Open Discussion Questions

1.  What areas of your life is it hard for you to let go?
2.  To what extent was God in your life as a child, and does this impact your current faith?
3.  Are there times in your life where you have made/ make it hard for your parents to take care of you?
4.  Does this same nature in question three come into play when allowing God to take care of you?
5.  Why is this in your nature?
6.  Have you ever experienced real thirst?
7.  At what instance do you come close to that same thirsting feeling toward God?
8.  Why is it so easy to quit dreaming like a child, becoming callous, low, weary, and lost?
9.  Has your hope remained as you grow? Why or Why not?
10. How does remaining child-like enable a blessing into your life?

## Chapter 4

# The Struggle Is Real

DAY ONE:

Take this class. Go to this school. Get this job. Marry this person. Have this income. Have this weight. Go to these parties. Talk this way. Our world is built with so many pressures and standards. Each generation is forced to mold more and more to the perfection the world expects of them. For people who have a perfectionist personality, like me, this often causes a great deal of anxiety. The stress and pressure to fit all of the molds that this world has is overwhelming and impossible. I have found that if you focus on pleasing this world and rising to its standards, happiness is virtually impossible. Aren't we lucky that we are to please the Lord instead of this world?

I was once having a conversation with a close friend who has a similar personality to me. She asked me, "What exactly is our best?" This question continued in my mind for sometime. How do we know if we are doing our best? This world is constantly putting focus on challenging and bettering ourselves. This world is constantly telling us to be the best. We have turned into such a

61

competitive nation. It is almost as if you are not the richest, smartest, most popular person, you have failed. We come to forget that it is impossible for all of us to be the best and to continue forward with this mindset is just a toxic put down. There is literally only ONE number one. How are we all suppose to succeed thinking we must each be the best?

This way of thinking is far off from Godliness. Believing you must be the best at everything has a touch of arrogance to it as well. This is no disrespect to you because I am equally guilty with this as well. Turning to scripture it is only appropriate that Paul wrote elegantly on this topic. Paul, the apostle who wrote the letters to Corinthians, was full of positivity, gratitude, and hope in his writings. How appropriate is that? Paul writes about God's standards verses worldly standards in 1 Corinthians 1:25-31.

> *"For the foolishness of God is wiser than human wisdom, and the weakness of God is stronger than human strength. Brothers and sisters, think of what you were when you were called. Not many of you were wise by human standards; not many were influential; not many were of noble birth. But God chose the foolish things of the world to shame the wise; God chose the weak things of the world to shame the strong. God chose the lowly things of this world and the despised things—and the*

*things that are not- to nullify the things that are, so that no one may boast before him. It is because of him that you are in Christ Jesus, who has become for us wisdom from God—that is, our righteousness, holiness and redemption. Therefore, as it is written: 'Let the one who boasts boasts in the Lord.'" (I Corinthians 1:25-31 NIV).*

Paul begins by stating how God's standards of strength and wisdom are above any of man's. The blessing God has given us holds that we will never be up to the worldly standards we are surrounded by daily. But God uses the weak, foolish, despised, to go forth and serve him. God created us with weakness to complete a greater task in his plan. A common phrase that I love the truth behind is, "God doesn't call the qualified; he qualifies the called. God equips the unequipped." God does not expect us to be perfect. God does not even expect us to be the best. He simply expects us to serve him and allow for him to supply our needs.

There is a simple beauty behind God choosing the wallflowers to fulfill his plan. God does not require the degree from the top ranked school. God does not require you to be in the best shape. God does not require for you to be in the popular group of kids. God is able to use you where you are right now. The blessing it is to not have to be the strongest, smartest, coolest person is beyond understanding at times. The creator of this entire universe believes you are perfect as you are (Song of Solomon 4:7). We are not expected to become the best or perfect in God's eyes. In fact, he asks us to BOAST in our weakness (2 Corinthians 12:9). God takes pride in each hair on our head.

He knows our struggles and our strengths and still chooses to place worth in us, whereas the world shuts us down and throws our worth out when weaknesses arise. Placing our worth and strength in the world's hands will inevitably leave us empty as you will never measure up. Placing it in God's hands will fill us with blessings and purpose as we journey in close relation to him. The frustrations will present themselves at times because as humans we desire to fit the mold of our society. I have learned this the hard way, as I am not only a perfectionist but am also a people pleaser. It is a hard task completely placing our worth in God and not having bits of it slip into society. I will end this with a verse that I often remind myself of when I have these slip ups trying to please the world.

> *"Am I now trying to win the approval of human beings, or of God? Or am I trying to please people? If I were still trying to please people, I would not be a servant of Christ." (Galatians 1:10 NIV).*

This verse is like a slap in the face for me at times. No sugarcoating. No beating around the bush. We are not to please man. We are to please God. To live constantly trying to measure up to man's standards rather than God's would not be an act of a devout servant of Christ. Slip-ups occur and God understands, but when these emotions of failure or worthlessness come when attempting the please the Lord; please give yourself that slap in the face. God loves you for your weakness and promises to use them. When you remain faithful and in relation to God he will use you for plans you could never have imagined, planned, or completed yourself. You are not on your own. You are not without a marvelous future. Just rely and trust on his plan and reasons.

Challenge: Ask someone for help on a task you cannot accomplish on your own and remember God does not expect you to be the best, as he will provide for you to succeed in his plan.

Memory Verse: *"But God chose what is foolish in the world to shame the wise; God chose what is weak in the world to shame the strong."* 1 Corinthians 1:27

## DAY TWO:

Weaknesses are something we all have. It may not always seem that way but everyone has that certain kryptonite that gets to him or her. It does not matter what the weakness exactly is; we all have them. Our weaknesses, like kryptonite for "Superman", are usually the one thing that has the full ability to destroy us each time they surface. Most of our weaknesses are even further complicated by our lack of control over them. Doubt, anxiety, and confusion can surface as we fight the humanly desire to be perfect. As Christians, this can be a worsened complication as well. I know for myself, when my weaknesses take control of me, I feel as though I am failing God. It will destroy my whole day even if it is just one simple thing. I convince myself that if I do not control my focus and emotions away from my weakness, I will not be able to serve the Lord. I convince myself that my weaknesses are of my own doing. Long story short, the weaknesses I have can ultimately destroy my value, worth, and purpose. It is hard for anyone to deal with weaknesses. Most of us choose to just hide them under the surface so no one will know they are there. Meanwhile, the weakness is able to haunt us and control our every mood if we do not take close attention of its power. This day we will be sticking with Paul's writing from the previous day in 2 Corinthians.

> *". . . Therefore, in order to keep me from becoming conceited, I was given a thorn in my flesh, a messenger of Satan, to torment me. Three times I pleaded with the Lord to take it away from me. But he said to me, 'My grace is sufficient for you, for my power is made perfect in weakness.' Therefore I will boast all the more gladly about my weaknesses, so that Christ's power may rest on me. That is why, for Christ's sake, I delight in weaknesses, in insults, in*

*hardships, in persecutions, in difficulties. For when I am weak, then I am strong.'" (2 Corinthians 12:7-10 NIV).*

This passage by Paul is a wonderful example of our humanly fight against weaknesses. Whatever you interpret the "thorn" to be, it represents Paul's weaknesses. Paul was a very intellectual and faithful servant of Christ. In these verses Paul was begging for God to take this thorn away from him. It even states that he pleaded three times regarding the thorn with God. God finally responds speaking of his power creating perfection within weaknesses. Even though this thorn within Paul was stated to be from Satan, God had a purpose for it all the same. Paul ends this passage with restored faith and contentment. Paul notes that not only in his own weaknesses but also in all forms of hardships he is made strong with God.

This analogy is a great reflection of our weaknesses. The thorn is a resemblance of how we treat our weaknesses. They can be big or small, deep or surface, and still have the ability to inflict pain on us without anyone having knowledge of this except us. Although it may not seem this way currently our weaknesses and hardships are in God's hands. We may plead and plead for him to take these from us. We may remind God of our faithfulness and the fact that we may not deserve this in our lives. It is so easy to get frustrated with God when he does not act upon these prayers. Our weaknesses may have come from Satan yet still serve a purpose for God. Sometimes our weaknesses are unfair and awful, this does not mean God cannot use them. Satan and God can use the same circumstance for different things. Satan willingly uses our weakness to frustrate us and lower our self-worth. We must have willingness for God to shape these set backs or hardships to bring joy in the end.

When you reflect on each of the characters in the Bible, they all have setbacks, struggles, and weaknesses. Does that inhibit God from using them in his story? Not at all! Some of these characters would not have come to experience the discipleship without these weaknesses. Sometimes it is our weaknesses that bring us to know God personally. Sometime it is our weaknesses that bring us closer to God. Sometimes it is our weaknesses that bring us to serve God. Sometimes it is our weaknesses that bring others to know God. Just as the verse states, *"my power is made perfect in weakness."* God's work does not end with our weaknesses. God's power allows for beauty to blossom out of the seeds of weakness.

When we pray to God fighting our weaknesses and pleading for him to take them from us, like Paul, we are forgetting God has a plan and knows what is best. An unknown arrogance compels us to continue asking God to take something away from us. Wherever you are today, whatever you are struggling with, and how ever patient you have been, God knows. God also knows of your future and all he has planned. Sometimes we need to go through these weaknesses to be prepared. Sometimes we need to understand these weaknesses to understand something in our future. Sometimes we need our weaknesses to completely change us so we will be the servants God needs. Now is the time to stop complaining and fighting our weaknesses. If you have given it to God, maybe now is the time to listen and continue to search with God for his purpose.

If we believe God knows our every struggle and thought, then why do we question his timing and reasons? When you continue to question God you will also slowly lose faith in him. Instead of questioning, it is time to truly listen to his teachings. The previous day we learned that God wishes for us to BOAST in our WEAKNESS. How is one to boast in something they have a disdain for? It is time to stop running from our weakness. It is time to stop making excuses for our weakness. It is time to stop complaining about our weakness. Now is when we must accept and bring glory to God through our weakness. If we truly are able to boast in our weakness and willingly allow God to use his power to bring perfection out of our weakness, then we will be in peace. We have this tremendous blessing to have a God who allows us to mess up, be weak, and fall in faith. God still see us as perfect with purpose. God does not give up on us. What an honor this is! Now the least we can do is to accept this blessing and bring glory to God with this blessing. The least we can do is be willing to take our weakness and continue on with our journey in faith. This is when blessings will rain down on us and our joy will ignite.

Challenge: Confront and accept your weaknesses for they are a part of God's plan in your life. Try to stop complaining or using your weakness as an excuse, but allow God to bring comfort and purpose to these emotions.

Memory Verse: "*But he said to me, 'My grace is sufficient for you for my power is made perfect in weakness.' Therefore I will boast all the more gladly of my weaknesses, so that the power of Christ may rest upon me.*" 2 Corinthians 12:9

## DAY THREE:

Every runner has experienced a time in which they ran until they grew very weak. They run until they felt their legs tremble. The simple ability to breath grows harder and harder with each stride. The muscles seem to throb with each step. They begin to feel as though if they took another step they could collapse but at the same time if they stopped they would collapse as well. They keep running and focus on each step as it comes. Soon enough things change. They catch their second wind. This allows for them to pick up the strength and continue on with the run. This gives them the hope they need to continue on toward the finish. Many people, who are not successful at running, have given up before the endorphins kick in. During the second wind, our strength is drained and our body takes over and carries us in our weakness. We lose sight of the pain we feel in the second wind. We lose sight of the fear of failing. It is as if we are lifted into a new autopilot mode as we reconcile our strength to finish. Our weakness is no longer our focus, our continuation and determination is the new focus. Our goal is the new focus. Our hope replaces our fear during the second wind.

Our weaknesses do have the ability to hold us down when we put a great amount of focus on them. Everyone has weakness, no matter his or her visible youth or strength. Every time we work through these weaknesses using our faith in God as our brace we will emerge from the situation with strength we did not have when coming into it. Ironically, our weaknesses do not always abandon us or become less of a pressing matter. We learn to compensate and over come the weakness, giving us a greater strength in the end. We learn to not allow the weakness to control us, giving us a different focus to drive us home. Just as the runner does not give up on his run when the weakness surfaces, he continues on until a second wind of endorphins kicks in to give him the energy to finish his mission. This does not mean the weakness completely went away, but he was able to finish despite it.

> *"He gives strength to the weary and increases the power of the weak. Even youths grow tired and weary, and young men stumble and fall; but those who hope in the Lord will renew their strength. They will*

71

*soar on wings like eagles; they will run and not grow weary, they will walk and not be faint" (Isaiah 40:29-31 NIV)*

This passage in Isaiah shows just how empowering the Lord's strength is when in the midst of weakness. God recognizes that we all grow tired and weak. We all have weaknesses that are alive within us. He is present to give us the strength and power needed. This passage states that those who hope in the Lord will renew their strength. This is the second wind we need to rise above these weaknesses pressing down upon us. Not only will his strength help us overcome the weakness but also allow us to soar. This reminds me of the feeling of weightlessness you received when you were younger and someone threw you up into the air or played the airplane game. To soar is to not be held down by your weakness. To run and grow weary is to not be paralyzed from this weakness. To walk and not grow faint is to not be paralyzed by fear but to continue on in confidence. Our weaknesses do have the ability to hold us down, but our God has the ability to take us into much greater heights.

The key word in this verse is hope. Hope is vital to not allowing the weakness to win. Just as the non-runner will give up once they become weak, those who allow their weaknesses to stop them will never achieve the chance for God to use the weakness. It takes a great amount of hope to wait and continue despite our knowledge of our weaknesses pressing against us. It is very easy to give up and state that it was not for us, yet God can do incredible things that we cannot image or complete on our own. Our reaction to our weaknesses reflects a great deal on our faith in God. When we give up or do not step out of our comfort zone, we lack the faith in God to use that situation. God created us with our weaknesses and still stated our perfection in his eyes. We need our faith to be strong in order for our strength to be renewed. Sometimes it seems as though we are waiting upon nothingness, yet our impatience can prevent amazing things from happening. Our strength can only be as strong as our faith. We cannot limit our God, and we cannot limit His time frame.

We claim so often to believe in his plan for our lives. We claim that he knows our future and will give us strength along the way. This does not mean a plan excluding things that we cannot do because of our weakness. This does not mean a future that will happen in our vision of the correct time frame. Our weaknesses test our faith; yet at the same time reveal our faith. We can allow God to use our weaknesses to further his kingdom and make us stronger. We can wait upon the Lord to give us the ability to achieve such strength needed to not allow our weakness to limit us. All elements of the strength in our weakness rest upon the faith we are willing to put into God's hands. Our weaknesses reveal to us just how strong our faith really is, and how much further it can go.

## DAY FOUR:

We all heard the rhyme when we were little, "Step on a crack you break your momma's back." Some of us may even be guilty of going out to the sidewalk and jumping on those cracks when our mom made us mad. So I have not written a letter to the sidewalk building industry asking if cracks made into the sidewalk truly are a conspiracy against mothers, but something tells me that is not the case. It would be a pretty radical thing, if true. Somewhere along the way a very smart, I am not sure what you would call him but for our sack we will say, sidewalk architect discovered that if you place cracks strategically along the sidewalk, the life expectancy of said sidewalk would be improved. Concrete, is a porous substance that absorbs water over time. This water expands and contracts with the changing in temperature. The expansion can cause concrete to crack haphazardly and eventually disintegrate. The very intelligent sidewalk architect realized that intentionally placing weak points along the design of the sidewalk would prevent disintegration of the sidewalk. These placed cracks allow room for the sidewalk to expand and contract throughout its lifetime without completely breaking. This is a good example of why perfection is counter to the laws of nature.

We are pushed from birth to strive for perfection and be our very best all the time, but a perfect person is just as illogical as a perfect sidewalk. We attempt to shape ourselves to be perfect due to the pressures of this world. Our perfection may seem that way from the outside, but as we absorb and change over time our insides build up. Just as with the water in the sidewalk, our being cannot possibly hold perfect under its pressure. The longer we attempt to remain perfect despite the built up pressure over time, the more inevitable is the fact that we are going to crack and crack destructively.

> *"It is God who arms me with strength and keeps my way secure. He makes my feet like the feet of a deer; he causes me to stand on the heights. He trains my hands for battle; my arms can bend a bow of bronze" (Psalm 18:32-34 NIV).*

We try so hard to ignore our imperfections, yet clearly God placed them there for a purpose. Our weaknesses can hold us back and prevent us from accomplishing the greatness possible. It is then, when we allow for ourselves to lean upon God in our weakness, that amazing things can come. No person is as strong as our God. No person is as loving as our God. No person is as smart as our God. When we try to please the world in our attempt to achieve perfection, we will never succeed. None of us are perfect. Our God is perfect. We, at times, allow power to go into our weaknesses. This power is destructive. It can cause pessimism, insecurities, and even depression. Placing our weaknesses in our God's hands allows for our hope to be restored. We are required to do as this Psalm says. We are to allow God to arm us with the strength and security to continue along our path. We are to allow God to provide our needs that we cannot provide on our own. We are to allow God to bring us to the heights that we could not achieve without his strength. We are to trust God in our weakness and for him to train us for what challenges lie ahead with these weaknesses. We are to trust that these weaknesses will give us the knowledge, strength, and courage to face anything that comes throughout our lives.

Along with our weaknesses helping us, our God can minister through our weaknesses. Weaknesses humble us. They allow us to connect on a vulnerable level with other people. Often I have experienced God using me in ways I could not believe by sharing my weaknesses or sympathizing with someone who also suffered with similar things. My weaknesses also help witness the power of my God. Many times I have felt so weak that I did not believe I could possibly make it through. After I had conquered that low point, I am able to look back at all the strength God had given me. I realize just how different my life would be without my God, looking back at those times. God can pull us through many situations through lessons of strength given to us directly by our weaknesses.

When I look at the weaknesses we all face in our lives, I see a direct relation to those cracks placed into the sidewalk. Each of our weaknesses is there for a reason. These weaknesses allow room for us to grow and absorb Christ's love throughout our lives. We are not made perfect from the start. We are made with cracks, and by those cracks we are filled with Christ. We are only made perfect in Christ's love and strength. We are not able to stay whole without him. If we attempt to stay whole and perfect without Christ, we will explode and fall to destruction. God knows our desire to be perfect, and by this knowledge he allows for our weaknesses to remain. These weaknesses are not to harm us in any way, like we often choose to think. These weaknesses are to do quite different. He knows we seek perfection, but perfection lies in Him. Our weaknesses humble us to lean upon his strength to be used and rise to greatness in Him.

Challenge: Look at your progress you have made from a situation that at the time you thought was impossible. Give thanks and recognize how God used your weakness to build you in strength.

Memory Verse: *"It is God who arms me with strength and keeps my way secure."* Psalm 18:32

## DAY FIVE:

Weaknesses play a funny role in our lives. They sit deep within our souls and we try our very best to hide them away. When a weakness surfaces, we feel as though we are out in the battlefield unarmed. When the world notices our weaknesses, our guards go up. Our weaknesses are something that can tear us down. If the world points to them all esteem is lost. Weaknesses build insecurity and remind us of all our flaws. You may be the most confident person but as soon as someone makes notice of a weakness of yours, you strike out in defense. We are fearful of the power in our weaknesses. We are fearful of what the world can do with our weaknesses. We hide them away, yet the world always finds a way to bring them to surface.

Weaknesses also have another power over us. They can take away our sight of worthiness. As humans, we see a chair that is wobbly and weak, we choose not to sit in it. It is unworthy of being our seat due to its weakness. We cannot trust it because it is weak and could fail us. This is our vision on what weakness means, and thus we begin to view ourselves in the same pretense. When we look into our weaknesses, we see unworthiness. One of the most common excuses that people use as of why they are not pursuing their crush is, "I am not good enough" or "I am not as strong as I used to be." We see ourselves as unworthy. It is not that we do not want to pursue them, but we see all our flaws and feel as if we would burden them. The statement that

78

we are our worse critics is most certainly relevant here. We give our weaknesses the power to strip all use and worth away from ourselves.

> *"Blessed are the poor in spirit, for theirs is the kingdom of heaven" (Matthew 5:3).*

In this beatitude, Jesus addresses those who are poor in spirit as blessed. Our spirit is the innermost part of us. It gives us hope, joy, and dreams. Our spirit is what gives us the strength needed to achieve something. When we hide away our weaknesses, we tend to shove them back behind our spirit. We compensate and hope that they will not overcome our spirit. Unfortunately, they usually do. When we allow for our weaknesses to strip us of our self-esteem and worth, our spirit falls under attack. The stronger power our weaknesses gain, the weaker our spirit becomes. How are these people those who are blessed?

Those who are rich in spirit, have full confidence. Their weaknesses are inexistent and nothing can prevent them from achieving their tasks at hand. Those rich in spirit need no help and are completely capable of full independence. Just as discussed in the following day, our weaknesses are used by God to allow Christ to fill us up. In our weaknesses God can exert his glory and build us to achieve greatness with him. Those who are rich in spirit never allow for this experience to occur. They do not need God and all his glory to achieve their task. Our weaknesses cause us to become poor in spirit yet the humbleness that comes by result then allows us to be filled with God.

Jesus continues on in this Beatitude to address "theirs is the kingdom of heaven." When we are open with our weaknesses and allow God to fill them, all of our hope rests in the kingdom of God. Our success is not limited to this world when Christ gives us the strength to overcome our weaknesses. If we attempt to stay rich in spirit, this amazing blessing is robbed. The amount in which we are able to accomplish is limited to this world when we attempt to do things completely on our own. During those times in which our spirit seems completely empty, the blessing of being held and rising in God's strength will bring an abundance of worth to our worthless selves. It is through Christ that any goodness shall come from us, and it is through Christ that all our worth is held. When allowing ourselves to become poor in spirit we are allowing God to pull us through, give us strength, and use our every purpose to glorify his kingdom.

Challenge: Confront and accept your every weakness. Stop hiding them deep within yourself. Allow your weaknesses to be open and allow for God to fill them with purpose. Realize each weakness can be used as a part of our God's plan.

Memory Verse: *"Blessed are the poor in spirit, for theirs is the kingdom of heaven."* Matthew 5:3

## Chapter 4: Open Discussion Questions

1. How are the world's expectations of us different from God's?
2. Which expectations bring on the most pressure we feel in our lives?
3. How do we bring glory to God in accepting our weaknesses rather than fighting them?
4. What way can your weaknesses shine God's glory?
5. Where is your faith when it comes to your weakness?
6. Do your weaknesses cause your faith to shake? Why is that?
7. How does God use our weaknesses?
8. What ways can you act and challenge your self to bring use to a weakness of yours?
9. In what ways are our weaknesses blessings in our lives?
10. How far do you go when trying to hide your weakness? How does this rob you of the blessings?

## Chapter 5

# The Limit Does Not Exist

DAY ONE:

My sophomore year I went through a very low period emotionally. I had fallen deep down into a pit of self-pity and distrust for everyone. I ran from many people in my life at this time. I felt as though no one could help me at all. During this time I had discovered my new closest friend to lean on. He came to me and at first I did not understand his ways, but as soon as I learned how he worked our bond grew. He lifted me up and allowed for me to express all this emotion and go to another world. He supported me as the pain overwhelmed my soul. He brought me to connect with another side I never knew I had. His name was Craig. Okay, well, maybe "he" was not a he but an "it." I developed a deep connection with my guitar, named Craig. I must admit, this relationship did not stay perfect. Sometimes when I would sing with his company our notes merged together to create music and praise. Other times, I would sing and one string from him would be flat. Then not only would he sound bad, but he caused me to sound terrible as well. I would get frustrated from this imperfect connection. Now, I could deal with this frustration by throwing him down and tearing him apart, but I still loved him deeply. I could deal with this frustration by continuing producing the pathetic excuse for music and mope from the harmony of the past being lost. And finally, I could deal with this frustration by ending our relationship and never returning to him even though he once brought great joy to me. Now for any guitarist, you know the ridiculousness of all of these ideas. I did as all beginner guitarists do and turned to a more experienced player to walk me through the steps of tuning the guitar. The guitar is an instrument that requires constant maintenance and tuning due to the depth and diversity of the sound it holds. It can get knocked out of its proper tunings from weather, change in temperature, change in environment, and age of strings. Sometimes the guitar needs retuning not from its own mistake but because of the different sound it needs to produce. It seems like I am tuning my guitar seven times seventy times a day.

> *"Then Peter came to Him and said 'Lord, how often shall my brother sin against me, and I forgive him? Up to seven times?' Jesus said to him, 'I do not say to you, up to seven times, but up to seventy times seven.'"(Matthew 18:21-22 NKJV).*

Maintaining relationships with people requires tuning just as maintaining a guitar. We must break all habits of keeping score of the amount of times we have forgiven someone. There serves no purpose in such. Can you imagine a guitarist who counted how many times he tunes his guitar as a measure of how good the guitar was and if he should get a new one? Some times the conditions people are under causes them to mess up or hurt us in some way. It does not always sound or look pretty. Is the proper response to bash them and throw a fit in furry? No! Are we supposed to ignore the issue as if it did not hurt us in order to hold the friendship? No! Is our only option to write them off? No! It is vital to communicate with them, tweak the situation so it works, and move on and enjoy the harmony as it is. Now sometimes the guitar may not be sounding correctly due to a broken string. Tuning the string after it is broken does not solve the issue. The guitarist must remove the string and replace it with a new one. At times, the damage done is very extreme. In these cases it may be best to allow the person to leave our lives. Once they have broken the connection with us we must accept this and forgive and forget. A guitarist does not hold on to the broken string and wish they could have done more to maintain the connection. The guitarist simply recognizes that the string is broken and throws it out. We must not hold onto these people who have broken connections from us wishing to have done more. We must accept that things have changed and move on. Tuning and changing strings are a continuous process and never will come to an end as long as you continue to play guitar just as forgiveness is a continuous process and is always a part of the Christian life.

In our relationship with God, we are the "guitar" and God is both the "guitarist" and "luthier." God created us complex with free will and many qualities just as the luthier makes the guitar with a depth of sound. God could have created us as a song flute; which does not need tuning or much maintenance but has no depth or quality to its noise. In life, we often choose the wrong path, make mistakes, or simply get worn down; in these instances God allows us to suffer the consequences of our mistakes or throws road blocks to guide us back on course. These are the times of our lives when everything is off pitch or out of tune. Eventually we cry out to God for forgiveness and help. Like the loving musician he is, he gets us back in step. Other times, God is shifting our life to enter a new phase in which we may need to play in a different key. No matter the case, God continuously pours out forgiveness and love as we journey through life.

When Peter approaches Jesus, he is like the new guitarist who is frustrated with having to tune his guitar. Jesus does not scoff out of Peter's ignorance, but truly reveals to him the continuous process required of forgiveness. Jesus was the experienced guitarist sent from God to set the example for the entire world of just how and how much to forgive. We will never reach our maximum state of forgiveness. Change within the path of our lives may occur, but forgiveness will never be of short supply. Just as our capacity to forgive must be limitless as well!

Challenge: Forgive someone who did something you have been holding a grudge about. Allow yourself to have peace and acceptance of the situation.

Memory Verse: "*'Lord, how many times shall I forgive'*... *'I tell you, not seven times, but seven times seventy times'"* Matthew *18:21-22*

## DAY TWO:

Ever since we were young, the concept of forgiving others was engraved into our brain. The first thing a mother does when their toddler is caught lashing out at someone is making them say "I'm sorry." It almost becomes second nature for us as we grow. We are taught to say, "please", "thank you", and "sorry." We learn very young to give and ask for forgiveness. Yet, as we grow old, why is it so hard for us to digest the full concept of this forgiveness? There are two ideas that I have noticed throughout my struggle to forgive and be forgiven that create a roadblock in the process. First, as a child when our parents forced us to say we are sorry, the words did not hold much meaning. Did we really feel bad for pulling the bratty girl's hair and making her cry after she took our crayon? At times, we also used these words to make a point.

We would say "sorry" in a tone that reflected our negligence to receive their forgiveness. Our hearts were not behind the words, and so when we received the forgiveness we did not take it to heart either. Along with this attitude, our society has a different view on forgiveness than our faith. The society we live in is centered on justice, which we learn more and more as we grow older. We have an attitude of righting wrongs. If someone does something wrong they must earn the forgiveness. If someone does a crime they must serve time to be punished. That is all grand and dandy for the worldly forgiveness, but this attitude of forgiveness will never be able to satisfy us spiritually.

The first step in mastering the ability to forgive others is learning how to forgive ourselves. The great puppeteer, Jim Henson, has summed up this connection of forgiving others along with ourselves. Henson stated, "Watch out for each other. Love everyone and forgive everyone, including yourself. Forgive your anger. Forgive your guilt. Your shame. Your sadness. Embrace and open up your love, your joy, your truth, and most especially your heart." It takes much more to forgive ourselves than simply the word "sorry". It seems as though when we are guilty of a transgression, we dwell on it. We get stuck on a replay in our mind. We continuously think with guilt and regret. Where does this bring us? We slowly tear ourselves apart breaking down our self-esteem. Gradually, we become so focused on this one thing that it becomes a part of our identity from which we cannot part ways. This develops into a cycle that is counter to forgiveness. How are we supposed to learn to forgive others and be forgiven when we lack the ability to even forgive ourselves?

The prophet Isaiah writes a great deal about forgiveness in the Old Testament. The book of Isaiah is in fact also known as the Book of Salvation. Isaiah speaks of the extent of God's grace in Isaiah 1:18.

> "'Come now, let us settle the matter,' says the Lord. 'Though your sins are like scarlet, they shall be as white as snow; though they are red as crimson they shall be like wool'" (Isaiah 1:18 NIV).

From this verse, we see God's definition of forgiveness. It is a forgiveness that cleans stains of the past. God brings forgiveness to us that can change our identity completely. This forgiveness is a forgiveness of transformation. As Christians, we know that the key to salvation is accepting God's forgiveness. Again, this goes far beyond the "sorry" of a two year old. We must go beyond asking for the forgiveness and both claim and experience the full extent of it. We owe it to ourselves and to God to not only learn selfless forgiveness but to also learn to forgive ourselves fully.

When we are trying to forgive others, we must forgive ourselves. How do we forgive ourselves? This first step goes beyond the thought of justice. We must abandon the ideas of righting wrongs. Once you have done something it is done. You cannot go back into the past and change it. What is done, however, does not define us.

It is also impossible to forgive ourselves without our own desire of this forgiveness. We will never be able to accept any forgiveness in which we do not seek, not even our own. When we forgive, it must be in the same nature as the forgiveness God has given us. If we hold onto any ounce of regret, fear, shame, guilt, or desire, our forgiveness will not be white as snow. Repentance goes along side of letting go. In allowing any bit to remain, we stain the forgiveness and it will not be washed away to the full purity God desires us to have. We must be ready to have God forgive us, forgive ourselves, and to then shut the door and walk away. Our full heart is necessary in the process of forgiveness. Sometimes we do not want to shut this door and walk away. Our heart wants to cling to these past deeds or thoughts. Sometimes we even lack the desire to give up these deeds or thoughts. When this is the case, self-forgiveness is virtually impossible because it reveals that our heart's desire is not there.

So many people forgive anyone and everyone except themselves. We must realize that forgiving ourselves is not a selfish act but a necessary act. To be an instrument of God we must be free from all sins. We must be able to walk with God, which includes his sight of us. This sight is one of hope and purpose. Lacking the ability to forgive ourselves will hold us down. We are not free to work in God's glory. We are not free to witness to others. We are not free to walk in faith. If we believe God forgives us all chains must be gone. If we are unable to forgive ourselves out of a lack of love for ourselves, we must forgive ourselves out of love and honor of God. We must realize that we are God's creation and God's children. Our identity rests in God, not in our past and present mistakes.

Challenge: Privately write your transgressions on a piece of paper and then burn it in a fire-safe manner realizing that God's forgiveness is complete.

Memory Verse: *"Though your sins are like scarlet, they shall be as white as snow." Isaiah 1:18*

## DAY THREE:

So many people view Christianity as rules and actions. I have talked with many teenagers who have abandoned faith simply because they want to enjoy their life. For myself, this is a hard idea to understand. My faith brings enjoyment to my life more so than anything else ever could. I wonder if these people have had the delight to experience the God that I have experienced. My God is one who turned water to wine so the festivities could continue. My God is one who took time for children. My God is one who was not afraid to oppose authority. My God is one who enjoyed dancing. He was not a wrathful God. He is not a jailor. He is not a critic. The God I worship does all things in love. In fact, he sent his son as an example of love. Many people feel as though they cannot combine a life of joy with a life of faith. The truth behind this belief relies solely on their channel of enjoyment they seek. Often people seek a self-destructive and rebellious form of enjoyment. In this channel, a faith life will not satisfy the desire. God loves us too much to allow for this self-destructive and rebellious life to carry out. When living a life by seeking this kind of enjoyment, the end result is far from enjoyment. When we live a life drawing our joy from that which God has given us, rather than worldly desires, we will discover a true joy without negative consequence. This type of joy is not only okay, but God desires it for us. In fact, it is one of the reasons he sent his son.

> *"Then Jesus said to them again, 'Most assuredly, I say to you, I am the door of the sheep. All who ever came before me are thieves and robbers, but the sheep did not hear them. I am the door. If anyone enters by me, he will be saved, and will go in and out and find pasture. The thief does not come except to steal, and to kill, and to destroy. I have come that they may have life and that they may have it more abundantly'" (John 10:7-10 NKJV).*

In this passage from the book of John, Jesus uses this analogy to address the Pharisees in regards to faith. He is speaking to a group of people accustomed to a religion of laws. These people were often too focused on worldly thoughts of their conduct than God's thoughts of their conduct. Their faith consisted mainly of reputations and action. As with many times in Jesus's teachings, he is speaking in metaphors. Whereas in this passage the thief spoken of is a wolf breaking into a pasture, in our lives the thief is the sinful nature of Satan interfering with our faith. The good shepherd in Jesus's teaching is God himself. Evil thrives on robbing people of their purpose, death, and destruction. Our God desires for us to live a life of fullness and joy. Without realizing it we choose between these two through our everyday actions.

When we desire thoughts of sin, we are opening the door to the thief. We are allowing the sin of the world to take possession of our heart. We are giving Satan power over us. When we choose to go get drunk or do drugs as a source of enjoyment, we are allowing for Satan to rob us of our health. The self-destruction of this sin damages our body and strips us of a part of our being that we cannot regain. When we choose to pursue sexual relations outside of marriage as a part of enjoyment, we are allowing our virginity and dignity to be robbed. We are giving up an intimate part of us that we will never be able to take back. When we are choosing a life of rebellion as a form of enjoyment, we are allowing the sin to potentially break a family connection. As we rebel against authority we are losing their trust and admiration. Although the possibility of regaining it stands, the farther this rebellion goes the harder it is to regain the relationship of the past. All in all, when we allow the thief to enter our hearts, destruction will occur even if immediate enjoyment is found.

Likewise, our actions can open the door for the shepherd to enter our life. Where the thief brought loss, death, and destruction, the shepherd brings an abundant life. This abundant life is not necessarily an abundance that our worldly standards can understand. It is not riches, popularity, or ease. It is one of fullness that nothing else could match. When we live a Christ-like life, filled with love, service, and faith the worldly standards do not quite compare. Although the joy is not so easily seen on the outside, due to the fact it does not always come immediately, the question of whether it is present or not is indisputable when experienced. This channel of joy is not one you can truly understand from the outside looking in. Not only can you be a Christian and have a good time, but your happiness is a part of God's plan. This happiness is empowering and lifelong, but any enjoyment brought by the thief will always be temporary.

Challenge: Spoil yourself, even if you may not feel as though you deserve it. Live today aware of where you happiness lies.

Memory Verse: *"The thief does not come except to steal, and to kill, and to destroy. I have come that they may have life and that they may have it more abundantly"* John 10:10

## DAY FOUR:

In life there are two kinds of people you often come across. There are the people who tear you down and remind you how much better they are than you. Then, there are the people who build you up, speaking words of hope and faith into you. It is very apparent on the effect each kind of person has on us. This is not an unknown fact of life. We may spend a lot of time trying to filter out the kind of people who surround us. It is smart to be sure your life is filled with the people who build you up rather than those who tear you down. Not enough times, however, do we look from the opposing perspective. It is extremely easy to play the blame game and evaluate the way everyone else is treating us. Things become much more difficult when we view how we are affecting others.

We must not get so bogged down in our own life that we are ignorant to the impact we are leaving on those around us. Did God surround us with his grace only to have us egotistically walk through life looking out for ourselves? Did God send his son to die for us only to have us stay in our own little bubble and rob him of the ability to use us? During times of hardship, it is easy for us to only focus on our pain, our needs, and ourselves. Our prayer life becomes almost begging God to pull us through the situation. We forget that from the moment God granted us his grace of forgiveness that grace is a part of our being, and it is next to impossible to keep all to ourselves.

*"But to each one of us grace has been given as Christ apportioned it" (Ephesians 4:7 NIV).*

Some people when they are saved attempt to keep their spiritual life and daily life separate. They have been saved and experienced God's love, yet do not allow their life to change other than where it is necessary to do so. Often we view grace as a glorious gift to us, which it is. However, having a mental state of the grace being ours cuts it short of a much greater blessing. In Ephesians 4:7, Christ's grace is said to be apportioned. Apportion, according to the Merriam-Webster Dictionary, is to "divide and share out according to a plan." With this knowledge in hand, we can truly reevaluate the grace we are given. Christ brought grace to far more than us, our church, or our country. Christ brought his grace to be divided amongst ALL his children. Now continuing on through this definition, his grace is said to be shared according to a plan. This reveals a plan for us. When we try to limit the grace to flow only through one fragment of our lives, we are not allowing God to work his plan out fully in our life. The grace we have received is supposed to flow through AND from us. We are to be used as instruments of grace. We are the hands, the feet, and the heart of God. We are to allow God to use the grace (which was apportioned to us) that flows through us to have the ability to be used to share the grace to others.

The unfortunate truth of being used as instruments of grace is the ability for us to both benefit and harm. We each have received grace. We must first choose to either allow the grace to sit in one area of our life, or to allow it to flow through all elements of our life. Next, we must choose to allow the grace to change and shape our lives. Both of these actions are necessary when allowing God to follow through with the blessing of using us as instruments of grace. This description is further made later in Ephesians 4.

> *"Do not let unwholesome talk come out of your mouths, but only what is helpful for building others up according to their needs, that it may benefit those who listen. And do not grieve the Holy Spirit of God, with whom you were sealed for the day of redemption. Get rid of all bitterness, rage, and anger, and brawling and slander, along with every form of malice. Be kind and compassionate to one another, forgiving each other, just as Christ God forgave you"* *(Ephesians 4: 29-32 NIV).*

When I think of instruments of grace, I am brought to a hospital setting. I think of instruments of grace being similar to the instruments used in a hospital. The instruments of a hospital have the ability to both heal and harm. They can save a life or they can further complicate the prognosis.

We can narrow this down to a single instrument to give an easier comparison, the scalpel. The scalpel is a tool that when in the proper hands has the ability to do miraculous wonders and save even the most severe illnesses. When we place our whole self in the hands of God and allow for his grace to flow through and from us, we are placing the scalpel in the right hands. We, the scalpel, are useless without being in God's control. With God, we can be used to heal the deepest wounds. Although, the scalpel, even when in the right hands, has the ability to harm instead of heal. If the scalpel is not properly sanitized and prepared before being put to use, it can cause infection and worsen the damage. This same fact goes for us. We can accept God's grace, give our lives to his glory, and allow him to use us, and still cause more harm than good. This is because we must clean our own life before we can spread grace to others. This concept is touched on at the end of Ephesians 4 (Ephesians 4:29-32 are provided, but I encourage you to read further in Ephesians 4 as well). It is vital for us to evaluate our manner, as we become instruments of grace. Now I realize, none of us are perfect. We will never get it all right. We are all sinners. All of this in mind, this is a very hard blessing to carry out in reality. But in these verses, it lists things we must be aware of in order to carry out grace.

The two main points I pull from these verses are hypocrisy and judgment. First, we must cleanse ourselves from all sins and ideas held before God intervening in our life. It is so hard to completely do this, as our human desire is to hold on to all things familiar. If we get stuck in a life hanging out with the temptations or even still falling to these temptations, we will not be able to show God's grace fully. Yes, we might have changed and truly accepted God, but to the outsider our life looks no different than it was before this change. Next, is the complete opposite of the first. Many Christians have a tendency to step out of this world completely when saved. They view this world as an arena that they must "fix." The sympathy and compassion fades and the relationships have walls disconnecting them. Judgment seeps in and causes our acts of grace to lack the love and compassion of God.

Throughout my walk with Christ, I have had my heart shattered from this infection growing within the church. So many people that I have encountered that turned their back on religion or have never come to know Christ all pointed to the same source: a bad experience with a Christian. I do not accept this as a reasonable excuse. This simple statement is so heart breaking. These people came to the church searching healing and help, yet walked away filling even more broken. This could be due to judgment, hypocrisy, or simply not being heard; all of which is unacceptable. We have this wonderful blessing of being used by Christ to bring healing and hope through grace, yet until we can let go of our own selfish or arrogant ways we will never be successful. We are the scalpels, and until we take the time to sterilize ourselves to the best of our ability, we will continue to infect even when in the right hands. Our actions determine the outcome of the healing. We can cling to the sinful lives of our past and bring infection instead of healing. We could cling to the judgment instead of love and fail to allow God to utilize us to heal. Or we can discard the mistakes of our past, humble ourselves before our God, and allow his grace to flow through us changing the lives of even the most broken soul.

Challenge: Suck up your pride and tell someone who you have harmed that you are sorry.

Memory Verse: *"But to each one of us grace has been given as Christ apportioned it."* Ephesians 4:7

## DAY FIVE:

Most anyone who is close to me knows that my choice sport is dance. Okay, I know there are the haters out there who love to argue that dance is not a sport. This is the exact reason I bring this very topic up. There is this huge debate that people love to get into discussing whether dance is a sport or not. Dance is not deemed as a sport due to the delicate side of it. Many people who watch dance and do not partake see it as a frilly, cutesy, entertainment activity. They see dancers as being girly girls wearing pink tutus spinning around to music. I find it funny because quite frankly that is the goal. Not completely, but in a way yes it is. Dance is to be executed in such a way that it seems liberating, eloquent, and easy. One must move with such ease and grace to complete the phrase as if it was one swift motion. Unless you have ever attempted dance for yourself, you will never know the blood, sweat, and pain that goes into every count of the performance. I have broken two bones, sprained an ankle, developed countless bruises and blisters, pulled many muscles, and practiced myself into a state of complete exhaustion all while at dance. Aside from the pain involved in dance, a great amount of strength is required. The vast majority of my classes are spent building strength. You must have the strength to not only do the very movements required but to go beyond doing them and do them in a way that looks easy and freely. When dancing you are not allowed to show a bit of the strain it may take to lift your leg to such height.

The essence of grace is not limited to the dance studio or stage. Some of the brightest people we are blessed to meet are those who inhibit these very qualities that dancers are required to have. These people glide through life showing liberation, eloquence, and ease. From the outside these people seem to have it together and are delicate in their nature of life. We view them fearfully weary of something coming in and breaking them of such grace. They seem delicate and innocent; almost otherworldly. These people generally are not as weak as we think they are. In fact, these people are often so much stronger than we ever could imagine.

The humbleness and gentleness these people have are not easy traits. Without strength the world would crumple them up, yet they are here and sending out blessings to all those around them with this demeanor they withhold.

> *"Blessed are the meek, for they will inherit the earth" (Matthew 5:5 NIV).*

In this Beatitude, Jesus directs the blessing of these very people as discussed above. For my full understanding of this verse I had to look up the definition of meek, as it is not a word I was completely familiar with. According to the Merriam- Webster dictionary, meek is "having or showing a quiet and gentle nature: not wanting to fight or argue with other people." Continuing down in the dictionary was an alternative definition present that stated meek as "not violent nor strong." This was extremely interesting to me. It is almost as if the dictionary provided one worldly and one Godly definition of the word meek.

On the second, worldly, definition it seemed as though Merriam-Webster took the non-dancer look at meekness. Just as the athlete watching a ballet recital smirks at the delicate ballerinas on stage; the Merriam- Webster dictionary equates the non-violent nature with weakness. They are not alone in this view; much of our world believes this as well. In fact, many young boys are brought up believing that part of being a man is fighting back when in reality the true strength is shown by walking away. To be meek, requires a great deal of strength to hold on to the self-control needed to abstain from the desire to fight or argue. It takes a great deal of strength to be gentle in the face of anger, sadness, and betrayal. The grace a meek person must hold true to is beyond any worldly strength known. The first definition holds a key word to the hardest part of being a meek person, "quiet." To be meek one must have control over their tongue and thoughts. It takes quietness to rest and hold grace in the midst of difficulty. So often the noise of the world overtakes our gentle and gracious nature needed to be these blessed meek children of God. Quietness is also required to be connected with God in a relationship. These meek people not only inhibit a quiet nature when facing the struggles of the world but also in their being and relation with Christ.

The most confusing part of this Beatitude is the blessing it entails. The blessing to inherit the earth seems contradictory at first due to our overall goal of the kingdom of heaven. When analyzing this verse, I am reminded of the segment of The Lord's Prayer, "on earth as it is in heaven." The meek people thus, viewing this verse in the remembrance of the Lord's Prayer, are blessed with bringing a piece of heaven down to earth. Although our inheritance is ultimately found spiritually and in heaven, we are promised this blessing as the kingdom comes down to earth. The meek receive this blessing while here on earth, for they are filled with the inheritance of peace and love through their strength in meekness. We may not receive the credit for our meekness just as the dancer does not always receive their credit for their strength, yet that allows for us to remain humble and gracious in this blessing given by God.

Challenge: Tell a friend family member just how much they mean to you. Never forget to constantly remind those you love that you love them. Seize this day to be quiet and allow for grace to flow out of your strength that does not always show.

Memory Verse: *"Blessed are the meek, for they will inherit the earth."* Matthew 5:5

## Chapter 5: Open Discussion Questions

1. How much forgiveness do we have to give?
2. Why is it harder for us to forgive someone after we have already forgiven him or her before?
3. What must you do in order to show grace?
4. Is it harder for you to forgive yourself or someone else?
5. To what extent does God desire for us to enjoy life?
6. Do you tend to find yourself relating joy to worldly matters or Godly matters more? Why do you think this is the case?
7. Are you an instrument of grace?
8. Can you visually see the impact that impurities hold on your ability to spread Christ's love? How does this make you want to act?
9. What blessings are we given through living in grace?
10. How does meekness affect your life of grace?

## Chapter 6

# Soft Kitty, Warm Kitty

DAY ONE:

Staying strong. Making it through. Just trying to live. So much of our lives have turned to focus on looking and acting like everything is good in our world, when it really is not. The seniors at my school often joke about how this year is a cycle of "just making it through this one week." We strive to keep up with the pace of the rest of the world. We do not allow ourselves to even breath at times. We paint masks of togetherness on our faces both on purpose and subconsciously. The world in which we get caught up in makes us feel guilty for not being okay. We hide our emotions when they are not those that would satisfy the people around us. We continue on in this cycle until our bodies are so backed up and held down by bottled up emotions that all we crave to do is scream.

This world has seemed to put Christians in this one little box. It is as though they expect us to have everything even more so put together and okay since we have such hope and faith in a God. It does not work that way, and this notion seems to create an even greater anxiety. I have noticed that there are two common responses to this pressure. One in which they give up and no longer care as much about being okay or acting Christ-like. The other in which they bottle up even more pretending to have it all together and loving life. Both reactions are extremely toxic on the soul. Our lives are not meant to be a drama production to satisfy the outsiders. Our lives are not meant to be perfect all the time. We are to live honestly in relation with God. It is as simple as that. This is not so easily done in practice amongst the outside pressures of the world. We are surrounded by temptations and images of how life could or should be. These are hard to cope with when not in a close relationship with Christ.

The apostle John addresses the honest relationship we must have with God in 1 John 1:5-9.

> *"This is the message we have heard from him and declare to you: God is light; in him there is no darkness at all. If we claim to have fellowship with him and yet walk in the darkness, we lie and do not live out the truth. But if we walk in the light, as he is in the light, we have fellowship with one another, and the blood of Jesus, his son, purifies us from all sin. If we claim to be without sin, we deceive ourselves and the truth is not in us. If we confess our sins, he is faithful and just and will forgive us our sins and purify us from all unrighteousness"*
> *(1 John 1:5-9 NIV).*

"God is light." When I read these three simple words I feel as though a weight is lifted from me, immediately. Simply knowing that God is light and there is no darkness at all in him is like a relieving breath of fresh air. To be in relationship with God we must step into the light as well. The light shines and shines through all of us. When stepping into the light without strong faith, it can, at times, be scary as if we are walking around with a spotlight shining down on us. Maybe this is the reason Christians are put in this little box. We are in a spotlight for all our mistakes to be seen. The next statement in this passage is key, "If we CLAIM to have a relationship with him and yet walk in the darkness, we lie and do not live out the truth." Wow. These words are shameless cold harsh truth. This is where many of us mess up in our walk with Christ, myself included. We will claim to have a relationship with God yet still be filled with sinful emotions of fear, guilt, doubt, or anxiety. We know the truth yet do not trust in it. We walk with these emotions bottled up and casting a dark shadow over our world. This act of walking with Christ yet living in darkness is the act of hiding our depths from Christ himself. We are required to live a bold vulnerable life with Christ. Vulnerability and honesty allow for the light to shine. When we walk in the light with Christ, John states that then we are able to fellowship with others and are purified from our sins. This is the moment our burdens are lifted and our community is strengthened. We must confess our sins. Pretending to be good, perfect little Christians is a deceitful lie in which we cling to at times. It is vital to be honest, accepting, and confess our sins with the Lord and then allow for him to forgive and cleanse us.

The truth in this passage is simple yet overlooked by most of us in our daily lives. So many times I have talked with people and heard them say they cannot tell God such and such because it is bad and they should not do or think that. It sounds silly when hearing, but many of us act this way on a daily basis. It is as though if we ignore the issue it will go away. If we pretend everything is alright, then everything will be alright. I am sorry, friends, but that is not how this life thing works. We all have our highs and lows; there is no preventing that. Christ does not want us to be this way at all. If you purchased this devotional expecting it to have the secret code of how to be happy and thankful twenty-four/seven, I am extremely sorry, but you can abandon that hope now. Trust me, if I knew that secret code I would be screaming it across the world not spending a year to write about it in a book. I am not that patient of a person. Life will always have ups and downs. Just simply becoming a Christian and growing in faith will not take away the bad. How we respond to the bad and good is something we can all work on.

This human tendency reminds me of playing a game of "hide and seek" with a toddler. The toddler will hide in the simplest ways such as: under a blanket, behind the curtains, covering their face, or simply laying face down. In their naïve nature and ignorance, they truly believe they are out of sight and hidden well. If they cannot see us then we cannot see them, correct? I think we all know the truth behind these beliefs. Do we spoil their fun? NO! We just let them believe we cannot see them until they are ready to come out of their hiding places. This is very similar to our relationship with God. As Christians we believe that God knows our every thought, pain, and struggle. So, when we hide from God due to our sin or guilt, we are the children in this situation. God can clearly see us hiding and knows we are doing so, but I found that the majority of the time, God allows me to sulk and hide in my sorrow as long as I please. It is not until I come out of hiding and confess these emotions to God that he is truly capable of bringing peace and healing to me. God knows where I am the entire time. Why do we hide? When growing in relation with Christ I have found the closer I am with him the harder it is for me to hide. When I do something I am ashamed of or hurts me while I am close to Christ, it is easier for me to turn to him for refuge. On the other hand, when I have fallen away from our relationship and am walking at a guilty distance, it is easier and easier for me to hide and avoid confronting him with my mistakes. When acting as the toddler we are doing exactly what John is stating in this passage, "claiming to have a relationship with God and yet walking in the darkness." It is so much easier to be honest with God when we are living our daily life in relationship with him and placing all cards on the table.

---

Challenge: Write a vulnerable letter to God. Confess anything that is casting a shadow of darkness on your life. Then destroy the letter as a symbol of letting it all go.

Memory Verse: *"If we confess our sins, he is faithful and just and will forgive us our sins and purify us from all unrighteousness."* 1 John 1:9

---

## DAY TWO:

As people, it is a slow process to build relationships around us. You do not go immediately from meeting someone to being his or her best friend. It is a transition of first meeting, then getting to know, next making connection, and finally becoming in close relationship. It is an insane idea to be super close to someone before fully getting to know them and all of their ins and outs. Many people (I hope many people because at least I do this), will go creep through the social media accounts of a new acquaintance and look at what interests them, how they communicate, and all the friends they may have in common. Honestly, in today's society, it is extremely easy to get to know someone. We have all of this information constantly at our fingertips.

When becoming a Christian it is so easy to get swept up in the born again rush and dive in headfirst. The love of Christ is magnificent and when you first experience all of its glory it is easy to get swept away. I am not saying this is bad in any way! To experience Christ and grow in passion is simply a beautiful blessing on its own. I am, however, saying that our relationship with Christ is built in similar means as those here on Earth. It is different in the fact that God accepts our every flaw and knows our entire story unlike when building relations with people, yet at times we forget our end of the deal in this relation. After experiencing God's love and glory we bask in his light yet what do we do in turn? Some of us change our sinful ways, and that is fantastic. Others may spend extended time ministering, and that is wonderful as well. Do we spend our energy seeking to learn and be close to God as much so as he does with us? I think this is one area that many of us neglect at times. It just simply does not come into thought when we think of our relationship with Christ.

> *"Fix these words of mine in your hearts and minds; tie them as symbols on your hands and bind them on your foreheads. Teach them to your children, talking about them when you sit at home and when you walk along the road, when you lie down and when you get up. Write them on the doorframes of your houses and on your gates"* *(Deuteronomy 11:18-20 NIV).*

Throughout history, this passage has been taken both literally and figuratively. In the Jewish culture they took this scripture so literal that they actually tied this scripture along with others to their forehead and arm. A phylactery is a leather box in which the Jewish men would attach to their foreheads and left arms with the scripture within it. This was a direct act under ordinance of this verse from the Old Testament. They also have a mezuzah that are a parchment rolled within a decorative box and attached to the frame of the door to fulfill the last request of this passage. The Christian culture has traditionally interpreted this verse in a figurative manner. We see this verse as a reminder for our minds and lives to constantly be in reflection and devotion to scripture readings. We learn memory verses to help hold the scripture to our common knowledge. Some Christians take on the practice of committing to read the entire Bible throughout the year to help encourage their daily readings in the scripture. Either figuratively or literally under-standing this verse, a multitude of cultures accept the importance of remaining familiar with the word.

This verse holds a very black and white request of us to stay emerged in the word. We are to embed these words of God in our mind through knowledge and in our hands through application. This passage instructs us to teach these verses to children not only in family devotion time but also in all aspects of our daily lives. It goes beyond the stack of memory verse and the prayer at meals. It is necessary for the scripture to not only be a study tool of knowledge, but also a heart of the structure of our entire being. We are to build our houses to hold true to God's word and reflect out his love. Just as in getting to know someone new, as we get to know the story of Jesus Christ, our relationship with him blooms along side. When one indulges in the word of God consistently, it becomes more enjoyable and fulfilling within our soul to continue along our journey.

Ironically our society has evolved full circle in some ways. Many people are able to take this verse both figuratively and literally. It is not too uncommon to encounter someone with a scripture-reading tattoo in today's culture. They might not have realized it at the time, but they are taking this verse literally and having the scripture placed on their body. I have found that the more I plaster scripture around me in my daily life the more likely I am to remain consistent in my readings. I write verses on my mirrors, school notebooks, sticky-notes in my wallet, by the shift of my car, written on my wrist or palm, and etc. Seeing different verses throughout my day not only encourages me but also reminds me of my relation with Christ in every part of my life. Along side of these little reminders, I generally carry around a pocket sized Bible in my purse at all times. This gives me the ability to turn to the word at any point of my day. In today's society the access to scripture is even easier than having to carry around a pocket bible! We have tons of apps and online sources of scripture and devotionals. The information to grow in the

113

story of God is constantly at our fingertips, just as that of the people in our lives. Funny how that works out? How much more of our time do we spend on social media staying updated on our friends than we do in the word staying updated on our God? That's a hard reality for us to face. This scripture, if applied to today's world, would be requesting us to open our bible apps just as frequently as we do "Facebook" and "Twitter," to speak God's message as frequently as we do the latest gossip, and to spend as much time studying the word as we do for our hardest class.

Challenge: Spend an extended amount of time in the word of God not only in quite time, but also through out your daily tasks.

Memory Verse: *"Fix these words of mine in your hearts and minds." Deuteronomy 11:18*

## DAY THREE:

To the outsider, Christianity seems like a simple act of going to church, reading the Bible, and praying. What an empty experience that would be, if it were the reality. Many people seem to not understand the "Jesus Freaks" that have evolved into this generation. I cannot explain how many people have questioned my naivety and innocence due to my "Jesus Freak" attitude at times. I do not mind because a few years back I would have said the same exact thing myself. There was a change in

114

my walk of faith when I no longer saw this world as the real world. This world is temporary and my heart belongs to a greater purpose than here. At this point, like many Christians when saved, my heart became no longer mine. I no longer long for my actions to be my own. I crave to glorify God. My eyes are open to see God in every inch of my life. God was no longer a segment of my life that I could place in a cubbyhole and label Sunday morning.

God is to be praised and experienced in more ways then simply those designated for his glory. Our lives are to be filled with God and all his works in everything. Not everyone is called to be a minister, yet through our callings we can serve and experience God. Our spiritual experience goes beyond our religious practice. We have the capability to walk with the spirit daily and indulge in the presence of God throughout every component of our lives. Are we truly taking advantage of this blessing? Many of us would like to say yes, but the truth of the matter is not always as pretty as we would wish. In reality we are cutting ourselves short of an enormous blessing, the blessing to live through and with Christ.

Paul wrote the book of Ephesians to address the strengthening of the Church he established in Ephesus. Paul notes an important task to strengthen the Church in Ephesians 5:18-19.

> *"Do not get drunk on wine, which leads to debauchery. Instead, be filled with the Spirit, speaking to one another with psalms,*

115

*hymns, and songs from the Spirit. Sing and make music from your heart to the Lord"* *(Ephesians 5:18-19 NIV).*

This verse is extremely relatable in the walk I take with Christ. I study scripture and spend time in prayer, but when I feel most connected with God is when I am living in his presence. But, just as in the beginning of this verse, if I were to fall into a lack of faith or into sin, I spiral down into this lowly place away from Christ. Knowing this fact, it is almost necessary to bring Christ into everything I am doing and to do everything I am doing to glorify Christ. When this mantra fades, my closeness with Christ falls in response. So many Christian will unconsciously break the Holy Trinity in their heart. They trust in God the Father in times of need and prayer. They follow the life of God the Son and strive to live in his manner. Yet, it is so hard for many Christian to truly believe that God the Holy Spirit surrounds them daily. It is as though the only time many of us allow the presence of God to overwhelm our soul is the moment we are saved. After we pass that point, we take control, commit to church, read scripture daily, serve our community, and pray often. That does not fill our soul in the way it craves to be filled. The element of spirit we experience when first saved seems to overwhelm us, bring forth emotions hidden deep within, and open our eyes to all of God's grace. This journey does not simply end there. So often we abandon the Holy Spirit after receiving grace. This does not mean the

116

Holy Spirit has abandoned us, though. The presence of God still surrounds us even when we are too arrogant to see.

Leaving out our journey with the Holy Spirit robs us of something magical. When we begin to allow the presence of God to flow throughout our lives the changes that come are amazing. We are able to do what we never have been able to do. Say what we have never been able to say. Walk where we have never been able to walk. And even when times are not the best situations we have been in, when we acknowledge the spirit with us, we will never feel alone; because we are not alone. We never have to be alone after accepting Christ into our hearts. He has blessed us with this, whether we act upon it is up to us.

All throughout my childhood, I have been absolutely in love with dance. A sense of release and pure joy comes over me whenever I dance, watch a dance, or learn about elements of dance. I often will tell people that dance is my soul mate, my one true love, something no one can rob me of. When I was younger, I simply went to classes did what they said and then carried about my normal life while practicing technique. As I grew and grew closer to God, I started beginning every dance class and performance in a silent prayer asking God to shine his glory through my movement, cleanse my soul through my expression, and lift me up in joy through my heart for dance. This allowed for me to experience God each time I danced. Even though, the dance was not directly bringing praise and

117

worship to God, it became so. The simple blessing of this love and passion continued to remind me of God's faithfulness and love. God gave me such a beautiful style of release from my anxious soul. I began to thank God for this and bring him into any environment because at the end of the day, he was the one who planned my life and blessed me with the little elements of joy such as dance. He was the one to whom glory and praise was due to. Everyone has those areas that bring them joy be it baseball, hunting, cheerleading, band, chorus, soccer, school, friends, family, pets, art, cooking, and the list goes on. All of these areas that we experience joy from are a gift from God. He gave us our talents, passions, and life. He shaped us and created us with all these in mind. Even though these do not necessarily relate to our Christian lives when we think of them, when we find release and joy from them that is ultimately from Christ. Christ is not in one cubbyhole that you go to when you wish to experience his glory. Christ is all around us in EVERYTHING. We give our lives to Christ, not just our Sundays and Wednesdays. We give our lives to Christ, not just our quiet time in the evenings. Our whole life and everything in between, we give to Christ to shine his glory through.

> Challenge: Take time to experience Christ through your talents, free time, and passions.
>
> Memory Verse: *"...sing and make music from your heart to the Lord." Ephesians 5:19*

## DAY FOUR:

How much sleep did you get last night? As a high school senior, this is a question I truthfully laugh at. For me, and many others in this society centered on always doing something, sleep is a rare instance. Or when we do happen to get sleep, a sound, peaceful sleep is very hard to come by. An entire industry has risen to tend to such a predicament in our world. We are very aware of the scientific need for sleep. Our bodies need sleep to develop emotionally, physically, and mentally. Yet, so many people, like myself, are stuck in a cycle of "all-nighters" followed by nights of tossing and turning due to anxiety of the day to come. Medicine, technology, aromatherapies, and white noise have all stepped in to help solve this issue. Aside from physical rest, our world we live in today is filled with a great amount of angst. We are constantly worrying about something and even sometimes worrying about not worrying about anything. Phew, lets take a breathe after that statement. Exactly, my point. We seem to run ourselves dry of all energy trying to keep up with the movement of this world. Our world falls into this cycle of all-nighters and panic attacks followed by long naps and lazy unproductive days. Where has the rest and hope fallen?

I have seemed to be blessed throughout the years with an amazing group of friends by my side. We all know the friends I am talking about. Those who we can turn to and vent about almost anything that is troubling us. They may not always have the answer to the problem, but they sure know how to distract me from my sadness or anger. Rather by their advice, sympathy, or humor, they bring relief and air into my life when I am upset and tired. These friends are only human however, and at times they are just as weak as I am. Sometimes this comes across as annoyance or just plain out hatred. Of course, these friends do not mean to be this way. We are simply trying to live life to the best of our ability, and at times taking care of ourselves is all we can take at a time. Our friends are amazing support systems at times of trouble, but they cannot support us and be the answer to all of our issues.

It is silly how often we turn to anything and everything before turning to the one thing we know we should have first. After all, Jesus himself has asked us to turn to him when he stated so in the gospel of Matthew.

> *"Come to me, all you who are weary and burdened, and I will give you rest. Take my yoke upon you and learn from me, for I am*

*gentle and humble in heart, and you will find rest for your soul. For my yoke is easy and my burden is light" (Matthew 11:28-30 NIV).*

In the beginning of this passage, God states to "come to me." With these words I visualize a young child. This young child has just fallen down and skinned their knee. They immediately jump up and before the first tear has time to fall from their face, they are running toward their parents. They want their parents to doctor them, hold them, and kiss it all better. With the words "come to me," I see Jesus asking us to come to God in the same manner. He speaks of rest, knowledge, gentle, and humbleness. In him, he will replace your load with an easier one and bring lightness to the dark burdens of your soul. This passage brings such a beautiful image in mind, similar to the one of the parent tending to the child. This is a straightforward, comforting passage that Jesus has presented to us.

If I am being 100% honest with you, this is one of the hardest verses for me to follow. Crazy, huh. This is probably one of the easiest verses to understand and take comfort in. It is not that I do not understand or take faith in this passage. It is actually one of my favorite scripture readings. So much hope and love is shown in these three verses. I simply cannot wrap my heart around them still. I know I am not alone in these troubles. I have talked with many people who struggle with perfectionism

121

and type-A personalities, and they all seem to have the same difficulty as I do. My personality is a "do it myself, be perfect at it, fix it myself" kind of attitude. It is extremely hard for me to let go of my imperfections and troubles. I want to take responsibility and fix them on my own. In my mind, I act as though God does not have time to deal with my anxiety. I also act as if I allow my pain or frustration to surface; I am showing a lack of gratitude for God because things could be a lot worse. I cannot explain to you why I think like this, but I know many people who have shared similar difficulties. It makes absolutely no sense. These thoughts are all wrong and toxic to our lives. I myself am working on this.

God does not expect us to have it all together. He does not dream that is the case. If we were to have it all together all the time, we would not have a need for a God in the first place. Jesus came to relieve us of this very pressure. It is as simple as us giving up our pride and coming to him. So many of us, like myself, refuse to take this step until we have fallen so far and hit rock bottom. I believe this verse is so simple and to the point because Christ knows we already struggle enough with it as it is. It is one of the few black and white statements in the Bible. "COME TO ME" and "I will give you REST." That's so simple and to the point. I think we need to work on not overcomeplicating the situation. Our God has instructed us to "come to him when we are weary and burdened." It is time to act this way. Time to trust in God. We

122

should be able to turn to God just as easily as we turn to our friends to vent. We need to remove this thought of God being too busy for us or the act of venting to God to be ungrateful from our heads. Jesus himself falsified those ideas. It takes a great deal of courage and faith, but it is essential to be able to let go of all that lies on us. The longer you hold on to a burden the heavier it gets. God does not want us holding on to anything. He wants us to lay it down upon his cross. The ingratitude is not in complaining to God about small issues in our life. The ingratitude is not allowing God to take these burdens from us. He sacrificed his ONLY son to give us this blessing of forgiveness, yet we hold our pains to ourselves because we do not want to be ungrateful? This is kind of a ridiculous thought once seen in that prospective. Any one who is stressed, any one who is suffering from insomnia, any one who is depressed, and anyone who is not fully resting in Jesus; I know it is hard, it is hard for me, in fact, sometimes it is impossible for me, but Jesus himself has asked for our burdens. He has asked to take on all that weighs down on us, and he has promised to replace this weight of the world with the hope of his kingdom. He has promised us rest.

Challenge: Spend the morning with that super cozy blanket and nice mug with a hot beverage to enjoy the beauty of a new day.

Memory Verse: *"Come to me, all who are weary and burdened, and I will give you rest." Matthew 11:28*

## DAY FIVE:

Many of us feel so disconnected from God during times of sorrow. Many of us even go as far as feeling abandoned by God when things are so low. When we go through difficulties our view of the world darkens, and we are pulled into this hole away from the rest of the world. The weight we bare grows and develops a control over us. I often think of "Eeyore" from *Winnie the Pooh*. Everything about his character reflected the depression he was under. The way he walked, talked, and thought all reflected the rain cloud that he was constantly under. Even the slightest detail, such as the way his tail hung reflected this darkness. Often, we get angry at our misfortunes, especially when they interrupt our happiness or contentment. Our world has developed a certain state of justice. Beliefs of "if you do the right things then your world should be good" tend to be very prevalent. This mentality leaves us frustrated and questioning, "why do bad things happen to good people?" I cannot even count how many times I have said this. This belief of doing and receiving is so implanted into each of our heads, but this is not a biblical belief at all. In reality, are any of us really "good" people? We can all agree that we are sinners. We do not deserve this forgiveness and grace that we have. So I think we can shake hands and agree to do all we can to throw that question of why bad things happen to good people out of our mind.

We all face cruddy situations throughout our lives. I will never ever, ever deny this from being truthful. However, we curse God when we are presented with these challenges, yet we proclaim he has a plan for our life. How does that logic work? Why would we curse something that clearly was a part of God's plan? This is when arguments come up and frustration is brought to the surface. Why do bad things happen to good people?

> *"Blessed are those who mourn, for they shall be comforted" (Matthew 5:4).*

This verse is so odd for so many people to digest. How can someone be blessed by mourning? We view mourning as such a terrible event. It is when you are your lowliest. You are vulnerable. You are weak. Your emotions are out for the public's viewing. Yet, here Jesus is stating that those who mourn are blessed. Anyone who has gone through the loss of something precious or experienced a traumatic event understands the severity of mourning. Even trying to think of this mourning as a blessing seems belittling to the emotions experienced. Imagine walking up to a grieving parent and commenting, "Oh wow, you are so blessed." This seems out right insensitive and insane. As with many things in life, this primus cannot fully be digested until the entire process of mourning has unfolded. Volumes of books have been written about the steps you go through when mourning. It is a long process and the blessing in which Jesus talks of probably will not be visible until you have completed the full mourning cycle.

Many of us, as humans, are stubborn natured. We are so stuck in our ways. We tend to run from the solutions to our problems. The most prime example I love about this exact scenario is break ups. They hurt. They are awful. Generally during a break up we spend the majority of this time eating ice cream, watching sappy movies, and crying to our friends. Our friends usually stick by us and tell us all the good that will come from this break up. Our friends tell us how our ex was not right for us. Our friends tell us how there is better to come. We here stories about fishes in seas. They are usually right, and we know this, but we still cry and cry telling them about how upset we are. We are stubborn, and even more so when we are upset. We refuse to accept even the things we know as true to be true. We refuse to even accept comfort at times because all we want to do is cry.

Blessed are those who mourn? Why are those who are so upset and broken the ones who are blessed? Many times God has to break us of even ourselves. We are stubborn. We refuse his refuge until his refuge is our only ounce of strength left. In mourning the weakness one experiences is so strong that the ability and will power to even open our eyes to experience the world is drained. The only way one can face life during mourning of any kind is by drawing all strength from faith. Times of mourning are when we experience our faith in full motion.

Most who have faced deep mourning have a moment in which they pull God into their mourning process. They question and even lash out to God in anger or confusion. This may seem sacrilegious to those on the outside of the equation, but in reality our faith is strengthened as it is tested. This time is when our faith is able to become real. No longer is it just placed in a pretty fictitious part of our life. It becomes real as it becomes needed. Eventually, in our brokenness, the only strength we have is the strength we find from God. We are forced to face God as a real being of power. We become an empty vessel in this mourning process and are only able to face the next chapter of our life once Christ is able to fill us again in his love and refuge. This mourning forces us to quit playing the fake game with God and to become real. This mourning forces us to break down any walls we may have built up and get real. Sometimes this is through anger, sometimes through tears, and sometimes through complete brokenness; no matter the means it is vital for our faith to come into God's hands in this time and blossom into his control.

Some of the most truly beautiful people in my life are those who encompass this very lesson. They are people who have experienced such heart break and brokenness yet still have an ability to shine their light to build others around them up. These people are strong. They are some of the strongest people I know. They have this beautiful ability to build others up even when they are down in the depths of despair. They do not do this due to faking compassion. They do this due to knowing and sympathizing with the brokenness of others. They have a strength that is not of this world. They are so strong because they do not hold on to the strength of this world. They know what it is to be broken. They know what it is to be vulnerable. Through this knowledge, they know the importance of refuge in God and allowing him to fill them with the strength needed to face the next day.

Challenge: Meditate in God's presence during today and allow for him to fill you with his strength.

Memory Verse: *"Blessed are those who mourn, for they shall be comforted"* Matthew 5:4

## Chapter 6: Open Discussion Questions

1. How does honesty and openness apply to your relationship with Christ?
2. How easy is it for you to be open with others? With Christ?
3. To what extent are we expected to study God's word?
4. How does the word of God shape your daily life?
5. In what ways are we able to experience God's presence aside from prayer and scripture?
6. Have you ever come to experience Christ in a way that swept you off your feet? Was this during a time of prayer and scripture or another means?
7. Are you fully resting in God?
8. What elements of your life do you rest in before you turn to God? Does this satisfy your need of refuge?
9. How are we blessed through God's comfort?
10. How can you shine a light into this world after accepting the refuge found in Christ?

# Chapter 7

# My Pleasure

DAY ONE:

Our ability to serve not only our community but also our world is a wide open door. Each day it seems as though another mission or service opportunity is created. More and more businesses are developed based on the sole idea of serving others. Our nation seems to be in a current outreach trend. It appears as if the amount of service organizations out numbers other organizations by a landslide. This is a wonderful problem to have if approached in the correct manner. Unfortunately, in today's "all about me" world, approaching service opportunities with the desired focus completely on servitude is hard to come by today even within the millions of opportunities at hand.

First, let's take a few steps back to truly understand what our goal is in this chapter. Servitude is defined by Webster's Dictionary as, "a condition in which one lacks liberty especially to determine one's course of action or way of life; the condition of being a slave or having to obey another person." Based on this definition, servitude is not only giving up your time to help someone or something, but to be completely without liberty and in obedience to another person. With this in mind, service should be a selfless act. You are to be under complete obedience. Who are you in obedience to? Well there are two possible answers to this question: the world or God. The difference is all centered on purpose. If you are serving for glory and recognition, then the glory is lying ultimately with you and the world. This scenario may sound ridiculous but has become more and more the common focus in our world. Although the opportunities to serve are vast, so are the opportunities to share your service. Many people go to volunteer and immediately "check in" their location to social media or upload a "selfie" of them serving. Even the planning of a mission trip has become a social media experience through websites such as "Go Fund Me" where you share all the good work YOU will be doing and all the pictures of YOU doing it. We have this new desire to not leave a single deed unheard. We want recognition and the world to know all the "good" we are doing. When service becomes a source of self worth and social acceptance, our service becomes a worldly act. To submit and give your self to the Lord's service glorifies God instead of self. To go unheard to simply fulfill God's calling brings glory away from the world and us and directly to him. The act of service must be submitting your self completely to God's needs.

> "*Above all, love each other deeply, because love covers over a multitude of sins. Offer*

> *hospitality to one another without grumbling. Each of you should use whatever gift you have received to serve others, as faithful stewards of God's grace in its various forms. If anyone speaks, they should do so as one who speaks the very words of God. If anyone serves, they should do so with the strength God provides, so that in all things God may be praised through Jesus Christ. To him be the glory and the power for ever and ever. Amen" (1 Peter 4:8-11 NIV).*

In Peter's letter, he gives this passage on living a life for God. Using this scripture I drew out three simple necessities to fulfilling in order to serve to glorify God. Beginning with verse 8, Peter states an underlying fact of loving each other. Love is a frequent command to all Christians. We are constantly reminded throughout the Bible to love our neighbor. Peter brings this a step farther in stating love covers a multitude of sin. With this knowledge we should accept that no matter our sin or our neighbor's sin, our love for each other should override all transgressions. We are all sinners. We must humble ourselves in service. We must not have an attitude of helping due to one being greater than the other. We must drive out any essence of judgment within our service. Our love should trump any sin that may have the ability to build a wall between the server and the served.

The next necessity of service discussed by Peter is to do so without "grumbling." Even if you are being forced by a friend or family member to serve, the act of service should be fulfilled with a joyful heart. There is no use in serving with resentment. You are taking away an opportunity for God to fully use you when you are not completely willing. When we choose not to serve with a joyful heart, the person we hurt most is ourselves. I am reminded of the blinders that are put on a horse to focus them on their destination rather than on the journey and scenery around them. A grumbling heart to a servant is very much like those blinders. They miss out on the improvements they are making to someone's life and the lessons that they could be learning along their servant's journey. Just as those blinders help a horse complete their journey more quickly, the "get the job done and get out of there" attitude of an ungrateful servant sometimes will get the task completed more quickly but without fulfillment and growth in either the servant or the served.

The very last element of service is one from which our current society has deviated. With all of the service opportunities at hand, we no longer view service as a blessing to the extent that it truly is. We set our service time into our calendar and plan it out at our own convenience. It is through the gifts, talents, and words that the Lord has blessed us with that we should serve. It is almost as though we have cut God out of our service opportunities. We are not sculpted to simply serve in whatever is the easiest,

133

safest, or most convenient means. Service takes sacrifice. Service takes stepping into trust. Service takes applying our gifts. Service takes much more than showing up and completing a task. God can use us in ways we could NEVER plan on if we open our heart and submit to him. If we do not do this, then we are cutting our opportunities short. If we do not do this then, we are no longer glorifying God to our full ability.

Challenge: Ask for God to bring an opportunity of service in your daily tasks and keep a watchful eye for the door to open.

Memory Verse: "*If anyone speaks, they should do so as one who speaks the very words of God. If anyone serves, they should do so with the strength God provides, so that in all things God may be praised through Jesus Christ. To him be the glory and the power for ever and ever. Amen*" 1 Peter 4:11

## DAY TWO:

Do I have to? Will I not go to heaven if I do not? That is not what Christianity is about! I cannot get to heaven through good deeds, so why do I need to do them? I have heard people use all these statements to avoid service in their lives. I will not lie; these statements are true. You do not have to do service to be a Christian. Your deeds will not get you to heaven. All of this is true and up to your free will. Service gives us the ability to be used by Christ. Service gives us the ability to bring others to know Christ. All this in mind is exactly why I view servitude as a tremendous blessing in our lives. Service and Christianity seem to go hand and hand, but not necessarily in the way that the world normally views them.

The things you do not have to do are sometimes the things our souls crave for us to do all the more. If you go through life only doing the required, you will not live as fully as others. One does not need music to dance. One does not need spice to cook. One does not need modifiers to write. One does not need colors to paint. But are any of these as enjoyable without the other? Is it as fulfilling to dance without music, cook without spices, write without modifiers, or paint without colors? NO! Sure you can do one without the other, but the final result of the combined option is far more enjoyable than without. This is apparent with Christianity and service.

> *"For it is by grace you have been saved, through faith—and this is not from yourselves, it is the gift of God- not by works, so that no one can boast. For we are God's handiwork, created in Christ Jesus to do good works, which God prepared in advance for us to do" (Ephesians 2:8-10 NIV).*

From the outside of Christianity it appears that to be a Christian you must be a "good person." This passage by Paul to Ephesians reveals this to be

135

false. It is only by grace we have been saved, just as stated earlier. Our works will not get us to heaven. YET, God created us to do good works. You cannot leave that part out of the passage. Sure we do not get into heaven through our works, but that does not mean God does not expect us to do them anyway. We do not need music to dance, but when someone suggests a dance we expect there to be music. We do not need spices to cook, but when we eat food we expect there to be spices so the food is not bland. We do not need modifiers to write, but we expect them so we can thoroughly envision the message while reading. We do not need colors to paint, but the colorful paintings are generally much more appealing than the opposing option. The works God has prepared for us in advanced give our lives a sense of purpose, meaning, and difference. In fact, some would say they are our life's purpose, meaning and difference. Without God's grace, we cannot do good deeds. Without God's grace we would not have been saved. The only thing God requires of us for salvation is faith, yet he has SO much more in store for us. Through His grace we are saved from the fate that we would face because of our sins. And likewise through God's grace we are able to truly serve. We do not become a Christian because we do good deeds, but we are able to truly do good deeds after we have become a Christian because Christ is in our lives giving us the ability to purely love and to purely serve.

There is a saying that you should not put the cart before the horse. Now just picture that scenario

136

for a minute. Before cars, how did vehicles move? Horses pulled them. Imagine how cumbersome and awkward a trip would be if you hitched the horse behind a cart and expected him to push that cart along. When we attempt to do good deeds for our glory, when we attempt to do good deeds with the desire to earn salvation, we are like that cart being pushed by the horse. God is our fuel that will energize our good deeds. Christ is the love that will touch other's lives. We must hitch Christ to the front of our cart in order to truly make a difference through our good deeds.

These deeds are much more than our own doing. If we truly believe God has prepared our good works in advanced, why would we not want to fulfill them? The last phrase of Paul's statement is quite humbling and empowering at the same time. Just think, the God of the universe, the creator of all living things, the beginning and the end, took time to create each good work for each of us. Does that knowledge not present arrogance when disputing the necessity of servitude? If we believe our God has a need, purpose, and plan for us to fulfill his will, we should hold our hearts open to take part. Just as we do not have to do good work to get to heaven, God did not have to create good work for us. Yet, he did create good works for each of us to allow our lives to have meaning. God wanted our lives to be more than a small speck in his creation.

Challenge: Offer to assist one of your neighbors or family members with simple chores.

Memory Verse: "*For we are God's handiwork, created in Christ Jesus to do good works, which God prepared in advance for us to do" Ephesians 2:10*

### DAY THREE:

One of the most common phrases within the Christian world is the phrase "blessed" (ironically also the phrase on which this book is based). We all try to count our blessings daily. I am blessed because I have a roof over my head, food in my stomach, family, talents, a job, a car, and am forgiven. Notice how many of these things are material possessions. What if our blessings have the ability to be burdens in disguise? So many times our emotions are stirred up because of lack of or the inability for these possessions to function properly. So many times our computers crash, our cars break down, our food sours, or our house gets broken into, and we respond as if Satan himself has cursed us.

On the other hand, sometimes our obsession regarding our possessions leads for us to worry about those who have to do without the "blessings" we have. This whirlwind our society has fallen into of "more, more, more" causes us to evolve our definition of necessities. Items that were once considered a luxury begin to be considered a necessity. This shift in definition of basic needs can be illustrated by the expansion of cell phone usage.

Not too long ago, businessmen were the primary utilizers of cell phones. Today, if you look around the average community of America, even pre-school children will be using an advanced cell phone. Before, it was common for most adults to not even own a cell phone, now it is surprising when a pre-teen does not own one. The government has even begun to provide free cell phones for those in "need." In a sense, even our lawmakers consider a cell phone a basic need.

Let's look at a verse that the majority of Christians know very well.

> *"Jesus looked at him and loved him. 'One thing you lack,' he said. 'Go sell everything you have and give to the poor, and you will have treasure in heaven. Then come, follow me.' At this the man's face fell. He went away sad, because he had great wealth. Jesus looked around and said to his disciples, 'How hard it is for the rich to enter the kingdom of God!' The disciples were amazed at his words. But Jesus said again, 'Children, how hard it is to enter the kingdom of God! It is easier for a camel to go through the eye of a needle than for someone who is rich to enter the kingdom of God'" (Mark 10:21-25 NIV).*

This man who approached Jesus in Mark 10:17 was seeking advice on how to enter the kingdom of heaven. He was a faithful servant of

Christ who followed all his commandments with joy. The verse begins "Jesus looked at him and loved him." The man came to Jesus with a sense of pride in his accomplishments of faith. Jesus knew he had love and faith in his heart. It was as if the man came seeking Jesus, wanting him to reassure him that he was a faithful servant and should have no problem getting to heaven. It is similar to when we go to our friends or family and ask them a question already knowing what we WANT them to say. Out of Jesus's love for the man, he could not do so. He told the man that until he was able to give everything to the poor, he would not so easily enter the kingdom of God. WOW, sell EVERYTHING and give to the poor. Why would Jesus ask such an insane thing of this man?

At first glance this incidence seems to contradict the true meaning of the gospel. Jesus is asking a man to DO something to get to heaven. I thought we were not supposed to get to heaven by works? The main focus of this passage is not the doing but the being able and willing to do so. But how can Jesus say it is harder for one person to get into heaven than another? At times, one simple mentality of this world can inhibit our faith from shaping our lives- our attachment to our possessions. As Christians we are asked to give our lives to God and to allow him to work through us. Our lives include EVERYTHING in our lives. Not a single part of our life is safe from God's work. So often we create a detachment between certain areas of our lives and God. It is like we are willing to pick and choose what God has control over. It is as if we are saying, "Alright, God is able to use my education, job, and morals for his glory, but my love life, videogames, and time are mine." Cold hard truth is that is not how this Christian life thing works. You cannot pick and choose areas for Christ to enter our life through. To be a Christian you must open the door for him to flow throughout your entire entity.

Jesus is more interested in a total devotion to God from this man, and not his items. Jesus, however, can see that this man is holding on to his possessions and riches. Jesus knows that this stubbornness will cause a roadblock in the path to submitting to God. It is not saying we must go sell everything and give everything to the poor. That is awesome if you have the calling to do so, don't get me wrong. The main focus is willingness. Are you willing to drop everything you love and have and give to God for his use? I do not just mean physical items. EVERYTHING. Your job, family, and anything that you possess are included in this. This is a no strings attached deal. No ifs, ands, or buts about it. God must have the ability to step in and use you at any place.

We must constantly be analyzing our life and all that is around us, so we may be aware of and accountable for anything that places a barrier in our relationship with God. When we become aware, we must be willing and able to let go of that barrier and give it up to God. God will allow happiness and blessings to still flow. We just have to be sure to refrain from giving our blessings the ability to challenge our devotion to God. Same goes for the other side, when our lives are low and not many blessings seem to be coming our way, we must still resist the urge for this to place a barrier in our relationship with Christ. We should take faith in our omniscient God, and trust in his plan for our future. Even though things may not be well or as we wish currently, he knows the desires of our heart and will not abandon us. All things he does through out our life are for our betterment, even when it may not be in our understanding currently. God knows the things that have the ability to come between our relationship with him. So when we are begging him for something and feel as though he is not answering our prayers, it is vital for us to trust his purpose.

Challenge: Donate to a local charity in some way. This could be through time, finance, or possessions.

Memory Verse: "It is easier for a camel to go through the eye of a needle than for someone who is rich to enter the kingdom of God." *Mark 10:25*

## DAY FOUR:

It is often said that a good deed is contagious. They can start a chain reaction of sending out blessings. This is one thing I love about the Christian community. Our good deeds being contagious are simply one thing that people know how to get right. Serving does not always take from us. We have talked about how we must bring glory to God through giving in service, to walk with Christ and serve go hand in hand, and to give up our ties to our possessions is to fully serve. All of these topics are surrounded by the overall idea of letting go and giving it all to God. Yes, this is necessary to be able to serve, but service is not all giving up. Often when I have served, I left feeling as though I got more out of it than those I was serving. Funny how things work isn't it?

When planning a mission trip, we are told to not go with any expectations. You must go with an open heart and willing to be used (just as we have discussed previously). You must go with the attitude of allowing God to guide you. It is strongly advised to not go into the mission field seeking to fix or teach the people. Partially because it is not our job to fix or teach, it is God's. Also, mission trips bring so much more to the table than that. God built me with what we call a "missionaries heart." I love to serve and give my time, talents, and heart to God's kingdom through service. My entire life I was this way, but it has become exponentially so throughout the past few years ever since my first mission trip. I discovered that God was able to speak to me through the people I was serving. Whenever I served, I left in return being served. You will find that after forming a habit of living with a servant's heart that every time you give to others you will gain much more than you have given up. The opportunity cost of serving brings enough blessings that the service's worth exceeds the outcome.

A more straightforward outcome of service is the joy that flows. When God is able to use us for his glory, an overwhelming since of joy flows through us. A since of purpose, accomplishment, and faith brings such a result. Many children are constantly asking their parents or caretakers for ways they can assist them. Even the simplest delegation of setting the table, watering plants, feeding the dog, and so on bring joy to their little hearts. They feel as though they have a purpose and a contribution. This makes them feel older and more valued. As we grow, we fall away from this desire. Getting a teenager to do such small chores is as though you were entering World War III. When we are serving others we must serve as a child of God not as a rebellious teenager. We are God's children whom are constantly searching for worth and value to his world just as children. This humbling mentality brings forth joy unlike the counter mentality. Ironically, as we embrace a servant's heart we will discover that it is impossible to serve without gaining growth to our soul. It is almost impossible to completely serve selflessly due to the fact we will always receive blessings in return.

*"Love must be sincere. Hate what is evil; cling to what is good. Be devoted to one another in love. Honor one another above yourselves. Never be lacking in zeal, but*

*keep your spiritual fervor, serving the Lord.
Be joyful in hope, patient in affliction,
faithful in prayer. Share with the Lord's
people who are in need. Practice
hospitality"(Romans 12:9-13 NIV).*

In this passage by Paul, the rewards and
needs of service are clearly present. The heart of
servitude is a genuine selfless love. This love is
beyond the noun love used often in today's society.
Love in today's culture is one that has no control.
You can fall in and out of love without the desire to
do so. This verb of love is in our control more so
than the noun. The verb love is the action of love
that we choose to or not to do. Paul is first requiring
Christians to back their service with an honest,
sincere love. To serve in this manner we cannot
paint on a fake smile and artificial care in our
service. Secondly, we are asked to serve with
"zeal." Zeal, as defined by Merriam-Webster's
dictionary, is "a strong feeling of interest and
enthusiasm that makes someone very eager or
determined to do something." The zeal is the
element of service needed to bring such contagion.
Zeal is the passion, motivation, spirit, and fullness.
Just as a team takes on the big game, they spend the
time leading up with pep- rallies, spirit wear, and
full focus. The spirit section then steps in and cheers
with their whole heart to pull the team through the
game. The spirit section of students paints their
bodies, gets loud in cheers, and brings noisemakers;
they go ALL out. This is exactly how service must

145

be with zeal. We must act with zeal to go full out in our service. Any act of service done half-heartedly is not enough. Just as to win the game, you must serve with such spirit to be able to serve with all you have. The passion that is manifested in zeal is further reflected in Paul's final request of the church. To serve with spiritual fervor. Fervor is the "intensity of feeling or expression" as defined by Merriam-Webster dictionary. Fervor pulls our emotions along side of the passion of zeal. Paul sums all of this ardent description of service with the simplicity of hope, patience, faithfulness, and hospitality of the action itself.

This servitude Paul states we must have opens up the door of vulnerability. Thus, human instincts truly get in the way of selfless, zealous, service. The hardest part of opening our heart in service is going into the service without walls. I recently have started working with a ministry serving the homeless of Atlanta. When many people walk into this situation, they unconsciously build a wall of judgment and disconnection from the people. It is as though they are not the same people as us. If they had not made, a mistake they would not be in this situation or if they applied themselves they cold get out of this situation. Truth be told, any of us could be in their shoes at any point of time. We do not have complete control of our circum-stances and at times they may spiral out of our handling. This wall of judgment and disconnection leads to a roadblock in our service. We must put ourselves in a state of vulnerability. This could be stepping out of our comfort zone by being on the streets of downtown Atlanta or this could be allowing an emotional connection and genuine care to flow through our service. Service requires more than the action. Genuine service is necessary for God's work to blossom.

Challenge: Spend time in fellowship with people in a nursing home, hospital, battered women's shelter, or homeless shelter.

Memory Verse: "Love must be sincere. Hate what is evil; cling to what is good." Romans 12:9

## DAY FIVE:

As we have focused throughout this chapter, the meaning and purpose of service has virtually been lost throughout society. As humans, we focus on right and wrong, fixable and broken, friends and foes. Much of our daily lives revolve around our opinions and ethics. At times this can drive us to serve, but not always with the right heart in hand. In the previous day, we briefly talked about how it is difficult for us to serve without judgment. The Church community can sometimes view the world through a narrow scope of black and white. The politics within our society and Churches cause for this view to become even smaller and smaller. Everyone wants to voice their opinion and how they would have gone about the situation. The motives behind this need to insert oneself into the argument change based on the emotions. At times this could be a conceited emotion driven by the simple desire to boost one's ego or pull the attention toward him or her. On the other hand, this could be a judgmental state. They simply want to prove how they would have gone about this situation in a better way or would not have been in the situation to begin with. We all, as humans, are guilty of each of these motives behind our voice of opinion. Yet, this is a toxic habit we have fallen into.

Jesus addresses a topic vital to the blessing of service within the Beatitudes.

> *"Blessed are the peacemakers, for they will be called children of God" (Matthew 5:9 NIV).*

Clearly our humanly approach to service has slowly fallen away from that of a peacemaker. Is this not ironic considering the heart of service is peace? Peacemaking could be the catalyst of when our service fills our soul as the blessing it truly is. Peacemakers must hold certain qualities to genuinely be peacemakers. These qualities are not always those in which we are comfortable or accustomed to holding. These qualities of peacemakers are also not always accepted or understood by society. Yet, to fulfill this role as the hands and feet of Christ we must strive to the best of our ability to honor such traits.

Many people who do not consider them-selves Christians argue that the Church is too black and white for them to accept. This is a very sad statement that breaks my heart each time I hear it voiced. Why, you may ask? Christianity goes far beyond following the rules. Yes, it is easier at times to stay connected to Christ when you do not sin, but that is not all it takes. Christianity is not a state of moral rules to follow or to impose on others. It is a state of community and accepting Christ's love, worth, and forgiveness.

Just as in the story of the adulteress being brought to Jesus in John 8, the mentality of right and wrong of the Pharisees is similar to how we act at times when faced with attempting to help a sinner. We must remind ourselves that only the one without sin may cast the first stone. I cannot speak for you, but that person is definitely not I. We must humble ourselves and realize we are just as guilty and unworthy of grace as they are. Yet, just as in this story, Christ still brings grace, forgiveness, and hope to us even within our sinful nature. We do not have to agree with the actions of those we are serving, but we must restrain from judgment. We have no right to see ourselves as right and them as wrong. We are all just as lowly as the other. When serving, we must do so with grace and love. When serving we must not do so with judgment. When serving we must humble ourselves to their level as we are all sinners. When serving we must not talk down to them for their mistakes. Service is all about sharing love and peace. Peace does not come with a set of demands.

We, at times, have an unconscious tendency to pick and choose our acts of service. In some situations we feel as though our service would not bring about a change or difference that is equivalent to our work and time. It is much more common for a person to volunteer at a soup kitchen or hospital than at a prison or a rehab facility. Some situations, in the human eyes, seem too "far-gone" for help. We all want to see the outcome of our service and will not apply the time to an area where the outcome may not be obvious. Why do we do this? If this was the way in which God decided who he would have grace and a plan for, we would pretty much all be doomed. Some seeds take longer to bloom and some plants take more time to tend than others. People and their salvation are just like this. Our humanly need to see the outcome of our service is selfish and takes away from the service itself. We never know when and where God may be using us to plant a seed or tend to a wilting plant. By us picking and choosing our service we are robbing God of this service. Yes, some service elements are scarier than others. If one allows for the fear to inhibit them, then God will only be able to use us in ways we can plan on. A peacemaker has no stake on the table. They serve to bring peace and peace only. When you expect an outcome in return for your service this is no longer an act of a peacemaker. Often God will bless us with something in return from our service, but this is not a promised item of our choosing. It takes stepping out of our comfort zone and removing our expectations to be a peacemaker. *"He must become greater, I must become less"* (John 3:30). This verse is one I often repeat to myself when stepping into service opportunities in which I do not always feel prepared or comfortable with. It is the key element to allowing God to use me for his kingdom in ways I could not do on my own.

In our society, alliances grow and gain control of our emotions and opinions on many topics. Just as in the lives of many teenagers, when a conflict arises one will side with their friends without hesitation. This action is almost one of bandwagon. You do not want to offend your friends and you want to support them. I am not saying this is unbiblical or wrong on any means, but when serving the Lord, this will inhibit our full potential as peacemakers at times. When siding with your friend simply out of alliance you are being counterproductive. To just say what your friend wants to hear does not always allow for the situation to be assessed properly. When a friend is fed up with someone and wants to fight, a friend in alliance will encourage this and support the fight, even when it is not a good idea. A friend who serves as a peacemaker will give them another point of view on the situation and pull them out of the fight. One of these scenarios agitates while the other brings peace. The first option is easiest and the friend would probably be more pleased with this support, while the second option is harder and can cause for the friend to get frustrated from the lack of support. Bringing peace does not always mean gaining approval. The difference is that the situation calms down and God's love and light can shine through when peace is brought to the storm. As stated in Galatians 1:10, we are not placed here on this Earth for the approval of man. Alliances and peace will not happen together the majority of the time. If your focus is on gaining approval of man then your servitude will be blocked. You must remind yourself of the glory and peace of God to be able to serve as a peacemaker of Christ and not serve as a servant of man.

Service is beyond the act in itself. Although viewing the world and all of its sin and brokenness can cause us to be motivated to serve, it is not always the right motive. Serving as a genuine peacemaker brings a blessing within that none can rob. Christ longs for us to serve with love and mercy. Christ longs for us to serve humbly and honestly. Christ longs for us to serve to bring glory and hope. Drawing our humanly needs, wants, and desires into our work of service can ultimately drain us of the blessing available. To serve with a Godly purpose will bring greater results than serving for any other motive. Serving with a peacemaker's heart, we will discover that our service is packaged with a greater gift than our action alone. Our service brings the gift of peace along side of our work. This gift is far greater than any action or help we, as humans, could ever provide.

Challenge: Help with a service project or mission in your local community.

Memory Verse: "Blessed are the peacemakers, for they will be called children of God." Matthew 5:9

## Chapter 7: Open Discussion Questions

1. How do we bring glory to God through serving others?
2. Explain how God has used you in ways you could not plan on your own.
3. How does service go hand in hand with walking in God's plan?
4. Is it easy to be a devout Christian without serving?
5. In what ways do our worldly possessions interfere with our faith?
6. Is there any one possession of yours that has the ability to distance you from faith or service?
7. In what ways are good deeds contagious?
8. What emotions do you feel when you serve?
9. What does it mean to be a peacemaker?
10. In our current society, are peacemakers praised, as they should be?

## Chapter 8

# Shelter in the Storm

Often in life we become lost and overwhelmed with the storms and clouds that seem to hover over us. This happened to me for about three consecutive years. It seemed as though life was taking this optimistic, joyful child within me and forcing her to grow up at a moment's notice. I lost trust in people I loved so dearly, lost control of elements of my life, and people whom I looked up to walked out on my life. Being a teenager during these difficult times did not improve my response either.

Just when I started to get my feet back on the ground, life put another roadblock in the way. In the beginning of my junior year in high school, I developed an unusual form of Hepatitis. I was rushed by ambulance to the hospital August 26 at 9 in the morning. I stayed in the hospital for about a week. I was beyond angry. I sat there with my mother one night when the pain medicine in my IV was not doing the trick and cried. I asked her many heart breaking questions.

Why is this happening to me? I already have diabetes isn't that enough? People keep telling me I am strong in faith, and they know God will relieve the pain soon if I remain faithful. How is that fair? If I stay faithful, God will stop torturing me. I do not see joy in that statement. If that were true, would he not have taken away my diabetes by now? Or would he not have prevented all of those painful events I just suffered through. Why am I here? My life is awful. I want it to stop.

My mom could not do anything to ease the pain besides saying she knows it is not fair, and she will be with me until things get better. When I was finally released from the hospital, I was put on bed rest for three to six months. That was honestly worse than the hospital. To give you an idea of how my life was before this; I was involved in dance, chorus, band, drama, honors studies, church youth group, led a bible study, worship band member, avid Starbucks goer, two jobs, babysat, and had about three to four different social circles. I had to drop all of those activities to rest in bed and recover for three to six months. I felt like I was locked in a prison. Many of my friends came to visit but soon they got too busy with school and sports activities. I began to feel like I was in a hole. I blamed myself. I felt as though I some how deserved this life since God gave it to me. I began to lock myself out of my friend's lives. I did not want them constantly worrying about me. I was not feeling better at all. Why should I bother others with this pain? This is something I just need to deal with and get over. As my bed rest came to an end, my friends began inviting me out constantly. I always found an excuse so I would not have to burden them with my troubles. The feeling I felt inside can perfectly be summed up by a quote from my favorite book (I read this while on bed rest and felt like it was about me- minus the romance side), *The Fault in Our Stars* by John Green. Hazel Grace states, "I'm a grenade and at some point I'm going to blow up and I would like to minimize the casualties, okay?" That was the position I felt I was in. The more people I allowed in my life; the more people who would get hurt as I get hurt.

Just a few weeks of being off bed rest, but still anti-social, I received the most heart breaking news. Waking up was always a hard task during those days. It felt as though sleep was the only place I could hide from the pain and heartaches of my life and body. This morning was the hardest to wake up to. My mom slowly opened my door and whispered my name. That was the first warning that something was wrong. On a normal day it is as though she kicks down the door pulling the covers off like a Drill Sergeant demanding my day to begin. I was then informed that my close friend Taylor had passed away.

I sat up to be sure this was not just a nightmare in my sleep. Taylor had been a friend of mine since middle school. We were best friends in middle school then drifted apart at the start of high school. The past two years we had just been getting close again. The fact that she could be gone was unreal to me. I asked what happened to be sure this was not some sick joke. My mom informed me, unable to hold back her own tears, that Taylor had committed suicide that morning before school. I felt as though someone had punched me in the chest. I looked at my phone to be sure Taylor or my friends had not tried to contact me. My phone was exploding with other people checking on me.

It took me a while to grasp the truth. I had lost someone I loved. I saw Taylor as one of my first real friends I had ever had. I felt as though I had abandoned her. I missed my chance to tell her how much she meant to me. I had not hung out with her since my sickness. I had taken for granted such an amazing friend who loved me. I had missed my chance to tell her I loved her. I missed my chance to listen to her problems. I did not even know she was going through something to break her as much as she was broken underneath. I was selfish. I was overwhelmed with my own trials and could not see the blessings that God had given me.

I talked (well cried) to her best friend about how upset I was with cutting myself short of the time I could have been with her. I told her how I didn't know if she even knew how much she meant to me. The friend told me that she knew I loved her and she loved me. She was always asking everyone about how I was doing. She felt bad for me and wished she could do more. Hearing that, I realized how ignorant I was. By isolating myself, I had taken actions similar to but not as drastic as Taylor. I thought that if I just left everyone's lives my pain would not hurt them. I was very wrong. The ones who truly love you do not have to see you daily to think or worry about you. Love and friendship does

157

not consist of only each other's presence. I thought if I pulled away from everyone's lives I could deal with my own struggles on my own, but life is not meant to be like that. We are not supposed to live on our own. God placed us within a community for us to develop relationships with one another to support each other. God did not intend on us to live a perfect life; that is why he sent his son down to save us. He intended for us to maintain a constant communication with him. Our difficulties were never supposed to be left on us and us alone.

Viewing these past few years I have noticed something to be true that I have always written off to be cheesy and cliché, our life is exactly what we perceive it to be. If we want a joyful life we must view our life with joy. Whatever you focus on in life that is exactly what your life will become. I was focused on my own struggles and not letting them impact the ones I love; in return my life became consumed with my struggles and I lost my connection with the ones I loved. This led to the worse case scenario. I did not just loose the time and connection with the ones I loved, but I lost someone I cared for and never got the chance to spend all the time I would have liked with them.

Now I am on a mission, a mission to live a blessed life. Life will never be perfect, why should it? We do not have control over what life puts us through, but we do have full control over how we respond. If we search through the clouds to see the light of God hiding in the midst of them, maybe we can bask in his glory even as it rains. This devotional has been driven by the therapeutic ideology of finding the blessings God gives during each day to begin to live a thankful, joyful, blessed life. Who knows, this could impact the way we see life and the way we live life to spread the glory of God's hope and joy. I wish to you my readers, that your eyes are always open to the blessings around you, even in your darkest days.

# Works Cited

"BibleGateway.*com: A Searchable Online Bible in over 100 Versions and 50 Languages.*" N.p., n.d. Web. 11 Feb. 2015. <https://www.biblegateway.com/>.

*Merriam-Webster*. Merriam-Webster Inc., 2015. Web. 11 Feb. 2015. <http://www.merriam-webster.com/>.

"Online Etymology Dictionary." *Online Etymology Dictionary*. Douglas Harper, 2014. Web. 26 Feb. 2015. <http://www.etymonline.com/index.php?term=bless>.

"Online Etymology Dictionary." *Online Etymology Dictionary*. N.p., n.d. Web. 26 Feb. 2015.

"A Quote by Jim Henson." *Goodreads*. Goodreads Inc., 2015. Web. 26 Feb. 2015. <http://www.goodreads.com/quotes/450966-watch-out-for-each-other-love-everyone-and-forgive-everyone>.